This Divine Mystery

Faith for Answered Prayer

Laura Taylor Cox

This Divine Mystery - Faith for Answered Prayer
Copyright © 2023 by Laura Taylor Cox

Scripture references noted AMP are taken from the Amplified Bible (AMP), Copyright © 2015 by The Lockman Foundation, La Habra, CA 90631. All rights reserved.

Scripture references noted NIV are taken from the New International Version (NIV) Holy Bible, New International Version®, NIV® Copyright © 1973, 1978, 1984, 2011 by Biblical, Inc®. Used by permission. All rights reserved worldwide.

Scripture references noted NKJV are taken from the New King James Version (NKJV) Scripture taken from the New King James Version® Copyright © 1982 by Thomas Nelson. Used by permission. All rights reserved.

Scripture quotations marked TPT are from The Passion Translation®. Copyright © 2017, 2018, 2020 by Passion & Fire Ministries, Inc. Used by permission. All rights reserved. ThePassionTranslation.com.

Ebook ISBN 979-8-9889289-0-4
Paperback ISBN 979-8-9889289-2-8
Hardback ISBN 979-8-9889289-1-1
Printed in USA by This Divine Mystery

Dedication

       To all the women of valor. You are mighty warriors who fight on your knees. You heap coals of fire on others by doing good for them. You labor with your hands to lift others up. Many times your labor is unseen and unnoticed, but the God-Who-Sees does see you! He notices your works and kindnesses and labor for others. My prayer is that this book will help you be more effective on your knees and spur you on to a greater knowledge of and a deeper faith in our Lord Jesus, the Anointed One.

Valor ~ khayil ~ mighty like an army

Table of Contents

Foreword

Laura has given us a true handbook in her book properly titled, This Divine Mystery — Faith for Answered Prayer. The book is encouraging, challenging, thought-provoking, faith-building. I have read many books, but I've never read one about "faith for answered prayer!" And yet, as I was reading Laura's book, I thought over and over again, "Why has someone not challenged us in ways like this before?" I am encouraged to reconsider the way I pray.

Early on Laura reminds us that prayer is a two way conversation, but how many times have we prayed, but took no time to listen, to see if God has something to say about what we just prayed?

Do I sometimes pray things that I really doubt will happen? Yes. Why do I do that? James makes it very clear that we are to *"ask in faith with no doubting,"* otherwise we are *"double-minded, unstable"* in all our ways.

And Laura takes those clear words from the mouth of Jesus and does not relegate them to the bins of history but challenges us to pray accordingly: *"Whatever thing you ask when you pray, believe that you receive them, and you will have them"* (Mark 11:24). Believe we receive them? How do we do that? We visualize the fulfillment and pray accordingly.

But how can we be completely sure that our prayers will be answered? When we pray according to the Word of God. When we pray His Word, His promises. Think of the words of Jesus in teachings to pray, Jesus said that we should pray that the kingdom of God will come. Can we be sure that it will happen? Yes. Why? Because this is a clear prayer command out of Jesus' own mouth. "But," you might say, "this has been prayed for centuries, often from people who are just repeating liturgy, and we still do not see the kingdom in its fulfillment." No, not it its fulfillment, but the kingdom of God is advancing! Often in areas that have been in darkness for centuries. John's revelation even lets us know that our prayers are mingle with angelic incense (Revelation 8:3), agreeing with those words from Hebrews 1:14, that the angels are *"all ministering spirits, sent forth to minister for those who will inherit salvation."*

I would encourage you to get a copy of Laura's book and use the nine chapters as a sort of "daily devotional," reading through a chapter a day, then pausing to pray according to what you just read. That's what I am doing. Laura does not lead us astray. She is reminding us, has reminded us of the clear words of scripture. I intend to take a step forward in my own personal prayer life after reading Laura's challenges.

Don Finto

www.donfinto.org

Preface

I've been a follower of Jesus all my life, a Spirit-filled believer for over five decades. I love mysteries. When I read Paul's letter to the Colossian church, I was intrigued by his use of the word mystery! Then he tells his readers what the mystery of God is! Jesus dwelling inside of us!

"The mystery which has been hidden from ages and from generations, but now has been revealed to His saints. To them God willed to make known what are the riches of the glory of this mystery among the Gentiles: which is Christ in you, the hope of glory."
Col 1: 26-27 (NKJV)

Writing this book has been a compilation of prayer facets I've learned over my life. I desired to write this to leave as a legacy for my GrandOnes. As I've written, and re-written, and written each chapter for the umpteenth time, I realize how far short I come to living what I've penned on these pages. I aspire for my prayer life to become His jewel of faith.

God has made me a jewel in His crown.

Zechariah 9:16
Malachi 3:17

I want you to know beyond the shadow of a doubt that you are the dearly beloved child of Almighty God. In order to have faith for answered prayer, you must be assured of your position in Christ Jesus. You are an heir and co-heir with Him. You are seated with Him in heavenly places. You are filled with His joy which is inexpressible and full of glory. He wants you to partner with Him in prayer by talking with Him and letting all your requests be made known to Him. He wants to partner with you in your life with your acknowledgement of His presence with you throughout each and every day. As your relationship with Jesus grows, so grows your prayer life.

Approach each chapter as a different facet in the jewel of prayer. See the beauty of the Scriptures and how they connect with one another. Polish each facet by taking the time to reflect on the "Practicing His Presence" section at the end of each chapter. By the end of the book, you will have a gorgeous jewel of prayer to offer to our Lord Jesus.

I am everyday.

Ordinary —

But with a twist.

I am unique

The only one —

Like a snowflake.

I am redeemed.

Image-Bearer —

Child of God.

In my everyday,

Ordinary —

I am victorious!

Laura Taylor Cox

Introduction

"Don't be pulled in different directions or worried about a thing. Be saturated in prayer throughout each day, offering your faith-filled requests before God with overflowing gratitude. Tell Him every detail of your life, then God's wonderful peace that transcends human understanding, will make the answers known to you through Jesus Christ." Philippians 4:6-7 (TPT)

I've been gazing at the Pacific Ocean off the shores of Waikiki thinking about the abundance and the infinity of Almighty God. We have access to this infinite abundance of Almighty God because we are in Christ Jesus and we have been created in God's very own image. This morning as I've been looking at the ocean, I've thought about how the abundance of the ocean is under the surface. We see the surface, but we don't see the depth of the abundance and the life that's in the ocean. All we see is the surface. And this part of the ocean that we see is just a drop in the bucket of the oceans of the earth.

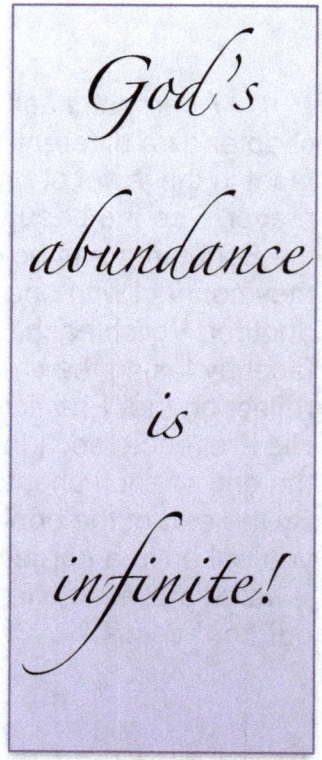

God's abundance is infinite!

The analogy of the infinite abundance of Almighty God with the oceans of the earth is shallow. It only goes as far as the depths of our oceans and they are finite. But with God's infinite abundance there is no end. So if we take something that's so enormous to us and then we add infinity to that, we get a little bit closer to the abundance of God. We would then need to add an infinitive exponential component of abundance to it and then we're even closer to the abundance of Almighty God.

Encapsulating this thought, we see only the surface of the ocean, but the abundance of the ocean is underneath the surface. So let's correlate that to our prayer life. In Mark 11: 24 Jesus said, "Therefore I say to you, whatever things you ask when you pray, believe that you receive them, and you will have them." When we pray, we're seeing and thinking surface things, like when we gaze at the ocean. Our longing is the abundance beneath the surface. Our belief has to be that the answers to our prayers are already in existence in the abundance of Almighty God. They are under the surface.

Call to Me, and I will answer you, and show you great and mighty things, which you do not know.

Jeremiah 33:3 (NKJV)

Now imagine that you are standing in the middle of this vast ocean with Jesus, Who can walk on water. This is in your imagination so you won't sink, but if you do, you can breathe under this water because it is in your sanctified imagination! You and Jesus are standing on the infinite abundance of answered prayers!

Jesus tells you to look up. Whether it is daytime on the ocean, or the ocean is glowing underneath your feet (how awesome would that be?) as you tilt your head to look at the sky, you see an infinite abundance of stars in the night sky. The Milky Way is a bright band of stars above you. The moon is

11

however you love it to be. Large crescent and low on the horizon, full and gorgeous, or maybe a new moon that cannot be seen at all. However you imagine the moon, it does not interfere with the twinkling of the stars.

You and Jesus are standing in the midst of His creation on a horizon where earth meets heaven. The infinite abundance of the earth's ocean is beneath your feet and the infinite abundance of the universe is sparkling above your head. Jesus is infinite abundance and you are the most important person to Him. This is the Divine Mystery! The eternal God is with you, in you, beside you in the mundane of your everyday existence. He goes before you and He is your rearguard. Even the smallest facet of your life is noticed by Him. You are a jewel to Him! He is your very present help, both in times of trouble and in times of peace. So much that we can find His peace that passes all understanding when those troubled times come. Jesus taught His disciples to pray "on earth as it is in heaven." Let's learn to pray so that the abundance of heaven permeates our lives here on earth. Jesus' desire is to be with you and to help you find *faith for answered prayer.*

The super-abundant God-of-the-Universe is with you in the everydayness of your life.

"The heartfelt and persistent prayer of a righteous man (believer) can accomplish much [when put into action and made effective by God—it is dynamic and can have tremendous power]." James 5:16 (AMP)

12

Chapter One
Why did God create us?

I can remember being in middle school and wondering what life was all about. The whole idea of God seemed so weird and something I just could not grasp. I was raised in church, and I believed what I was taught, but I still had a huge, "But WHY?" in the back of my head. Not all the time, but sometimes, when I would look up in the night sky and feel so very small, I would ask, "Why? Why would God do all this?" In this chapter, we're going to talk about this "why" and the "why" of the cross. Why did Jesus have to die? We're going to touch on prayer, belief, and ultimately how we can walk more connected with Jesus than we've ever walked before.

> "In the beginning God created the heavens and the earth." Genesis 1:1 (NKJV)

Jesus, the Alpha and Omega, the Beginning and the Ending, stood on the precipice of eternity past and said, "Light be!" And it was! And it was a very good thing! But why did God create in the first place?

Think about the time before Genesis 1, before God spoke our Universe into existence. Was God Almighty in need of anything? Was there any lack in the realm in which He existed? If you think about Almighty God before He created the universe, there was not lack, there was no need. He was already in the heavenly realm. He is complete in and of Himself. The Triune Almighty; God the Father, God the Son, and God the Holy Spirit. Unexplainable. All-powerful. Omnipotent. From Everlasting to Everlasting. Without beginning and without end. Did the Almighty God *need* anything? No! Absolutely not! Almighty God did not *need* anything. But I will submit to you that He *wanted* something —us. You and me.

> "Let Us make humans in Our image, according to Our likeness; let them have dominion over the fish of the sea, over the birds of the air, over the cattle, over all the earth and over every creeping thing that creeps on the earth." Genesis 1:26 (NKJV)

Humans are the only beings created in His image. He wanted family. He wanted us so much, that when He counted what it would cost Him to create the Universe, He decided that giving His life for us would be worth it! Revelation tells us that He created everything for His pleasure.

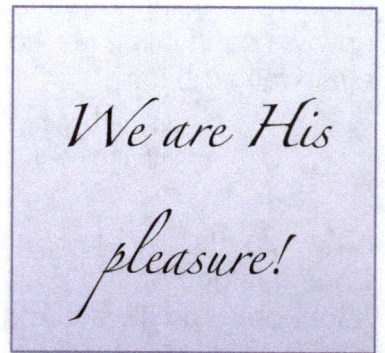

We are His pleasure!

> "You are worthy, our Lord and God, to receive glory, honor, and power, for you created all things, and for your pleasure they were created and exist."
> Revelation 5:12 (TPT)

The Word also tells us that before anything was created, before the first light in our universe blasted into existence, God the Father, God the Son, and God the Holy Spirit counted the cost.

> "This was part of God's plan, for he (Jesus)

14

was chosen and destined for this *before the foundation of the earth was laid, ...*"

1 Peter 1:20 (TPT) (emphasis mine)

Also in Revelation there is a verse that talks about the book of life of the Lamb, meaning Jesus, and that Lamb knew He would be sacrificed before the earth was even created.

"the Lamb slain *from the foundation of the world...*" Revelation 13:8 (NKJV) (emphasis mine)

So before He was the Beginning, He knew He would be the Ending. The cross did not take Him by surprise. It was His plan all along. According to these Scriptures, Jesus knew He would suffer and die before He said, "Light be!"

The first chapter of Colossians tells us that all things were created through Jesus and there is nothing that was created without Him.

God wanted us to be His family!

"He (Jesus) is the image of the invisible God, the firstborn over all creation. For by Him all things were created that are in heaven and that are on earth, visible and invisible, whether thrones or dominions or principalities or powers. All things were created through Him and for Him."

Col 1:15-16 (NKJV)

Make no mistake, Jesus, the Omnipotent God Who knew everything, knew what it would cost Him to create humanity

15

in His image. Even knowing what lay before Him, He said, "Let there be light!" anyway. He *wanted* family! He wanted us! We are His joy!

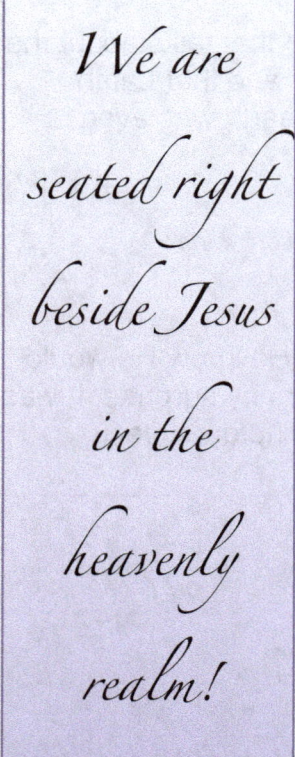

We are seated right beside Jesus in the heavenly realm!

"…who for the joy that was set before Him endured the cross, despising the shame…"
Heb 12:2 (NKJV)

Jesus wanted us so much that He submitted Himself to the cross so that we could live with Him forever. He loved us so much that He died and rose again so that we could have everlasting life. This is an amazing thought. This is a very humbling thought. This was His plan from the beginning and He executed it perfectly! This Scripture in Hebrews tells us where Jesus ended up after His resurrection.

"and (Jesus) has sat down at the right hand of the throne of God." Hebrews 12:2 (NKJV)

The Alpha knew that He was also the Omega - the Beginning had an Ending—AND He knew that He would accomplish what He set out to do. The Alpha knew the Omega would work! There were no if's, and's, or but's about it. The finished work of the cross was sealed in eternity before our time began. Jesus is the Alpha and the Omega. He is seated at the right hand of God, the Father. It is this throne room that we can boldly access and let our requests be made known! We can enter right into the throne room of Almighty God any time we want, because He has opened His throne room to us and He has invited us in! But, it does get a bit better than that! Several times in the New Testament it says that Jesus has raised us up and seated us with Him in the heavenly places!

"Let us therefore come boldly to the throne of grace, that we may obtain mercy and find grace to help in time of need." Hebrews 4:16 (NKJV)

"If then you were raised with Christ, seek those things which are above, where Christ is, sitting at the right hand of God." Col 3:1 (NKJV)

"…and raised us up together, and made us sit together in the heavenly places in Christ Jesus," Eph 2:6 (NKJV)

"He raised us up with Christ the exalted One, and we ascended with him into the glorious perfection and authority of the heavenly realm, for we are now co-seated as one with Christ!"
Eph 2:6 (TPT)

Where is Jesus seated? (At the right hand of God!) Where did He raise us to? (Seated with Him in heavenly places.) Where are we seated with Him? (At the right hand of God!) The Psalmist had a glimpse into this wonderful position we have in Christ.

At God's right hand are pleasures forevermore

"You will show me the path of life; In Your presence is fullness of joy; At Your right hand are pleasures forevermore."

Psalm 16:11 (NKJV)

We have seen that after Jesus ascended into heaven He sat down at the right hand of God. At God's right hand are pleasures forevermore! Then we looked at Scriptures that say we are seated with Jesus in the heavenly realm. At God's right hand are pleasures forevermore! For His pleasure all things were created. We were created in His image. The Passion Translation uses the term "image-bearers" when talking about humans. We, His image-bearers, are seated with Jesus in heavenly places at the right hand of God where His pleasures are forevermore! We are God's pleasures!

On February 11, 1975, I became a committed follower of Jesus. I believed in Him all my life, but I didn't know how to follow Him. I began to see life in a whole new way. When I would look up into the night sky, I no longer asked "Who are You?" or "Why did You create all this?" My mind would just be overwhelmed with the infinite love of God. His mercy would overtake me. I knew that He created everything. I knew He stood outside of time and space. I also knew that He stood beside me and lived inside me. The Infinite, Almighty Creator knew me and loved me!

What is prayer?

In its most simplistic definition, prayer is communication with God. He's Almighty God, Creator of heaven and earth, so why would He even care about our concerns—the things we pray for—in the big scope and sequence of the Universe? Good question! It's fairly obvious why we want to talk with God, but why would He want to be in communication with us? We are His pleasure! He loves to communicate with us!

If we're seated with Jesus in heavenly places, and Jesus is right next to the Father God Almighty, it seems fairly easy to be able to talk with Him. Does this mean that we can lean across Jesus and talk directly to Almighty God? Well, yes! To have a conversation with God. To listen to Him. To be in relationship with the One Who created us in order to be in relationship with Him! So, how often should we pray? In the Garden of Gethsemane, Jesus prayed three times. The Psalmist mentioned seven times a day. The Apostle Paul said to pray constantly! Can we pray too much? Nope!

"So He left them, went away again, and prayed the third time, saying the same words." Matthew 26:44 (NKJV)

"Seven times a day I praise You, because of Your righteous judgments." Psalm 119:164 (NKJV)

"Rejoice always, pray without ceasing, in everything give thanks; for this is the will of God in Christ Jesus for you."
1 Thessalonians 5:16-18 (NKJV)

We will delve into this Thessalonians verse in a later chapter, but for now we are concentrating on the idea of praying without ceasing. Our lives should be an attitude of prayer. Think about it this way. You're on a road trip with a family member or a very close friend. You can sit in silence and enjoy the journey. Or you can talk. Or listen to music. One person starts a conversation and it continues for a while. There is no constant chatter, nor do you discuss the plans for the day and never say another word to one another until time for bed. Throughout the day you converse with your friend. You are always aware of your friend in the vehicle with you. That's a good analogy for praying without ceasing.

It is such a wonderful feeling to pray for something and then see that prayer answered in the affirmative. Sometimes we pray for things—our list—and then we get busy in life and don't really notice if and when those prayers are answered. Then there are the times when we pray for a specific thing and the opposite happens. Oh my! Sometimes it feels that we have to catch God on a good day to get our prayers answered! But that's not the case!

Do you Believe?

Do you believe in God? Really examine your thoughts and feelings that come up when you ask yourself that question. **Do you believe in God?** If you are unsure then ask Him to reveal Himself to you. I believe one of the most honest prayers in the Bible was the distraught Dad who, with tears in his eyes, cried out to Jesus,

"Lord, I believe; help my unbelief!"
Mark 9:24 (NKJV)

That was an anguished cry from his gut. We all have places of unbelief hidden deep inside that we do not want to surface. But if we never become aware of them, if we never acknowledge them, if we pretend that they don't exist in us, then we can never deal with them and rid ourselves of them. May we, like this Dad 2000 years ago, cry out to our Lord and Savior, "Jesus! I believe! Help my unbelief!" Now, back to the question. Do you believe in God?

"But without faith it is impossible to please Him, for he who comes to God must believe that He is, and that He is a rewarder of those who diligently seek Him." Heb 11:6 (NKJV)

20

This verse says that God rewards those who believe in Him and diligently seek Him! Isn't that awesome? So you believe that God exists, do you believe that He will reward you because you believe in Him and seek after Him? We've been taught that it is better to give than to receive. That came from Almighty God who is the Great Giver. Will you allow Him to reward you for believing in Him and seeking Him so that you will then be able to follow His footsteps into true giving? I am convinced that you cannot be a giver until you learn to receive. If it's more blessed to give, then everyone wants to be more blessed. But there has to be a receiver. That is the humble part of this transaction. If you can't humble yourself to receive, you can't give in humility.

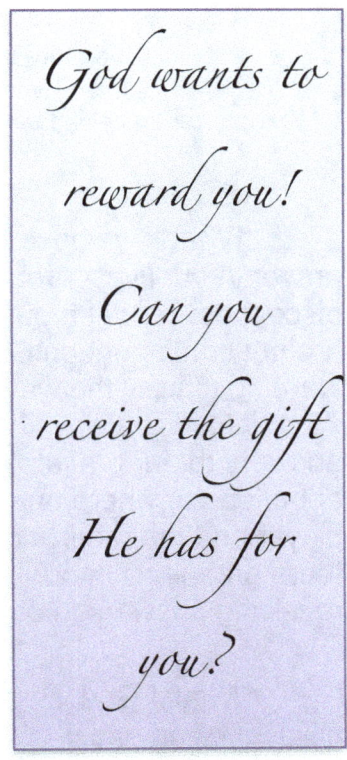

God wants to reward you! Can you receive the gift He has for you?

One of my favorite books is "The 5 Love Languages" by Gary Chapman. I highly recommend this book for every single relationship you are in. One of my top love languages is gifts. I love to shop for gifts for others. I also love to receive gifts. When I really saw this Scripture, that God is a rewarder of those who seek Him, it spoke to my love language of gifts! This is one of the Scriptures that I treasure in my heart.

Another one of the verses we are going to discuss several times, is a Scripture in which Jesus is teaching His disciples on prayer. In fact, I consider it the anchor Scripture where faith for answered prayer is concerned.

> "Therefore I say to you, whatever things you ask when you pray, believe that you receive them, and you will have them."
> Mark 11:24 (NKJV)

What if we have thwarted God's reward of answered prayer in our lives through hidden unbelief? What if the disconnect between our prayers and answers to our prayers are not contingent on God having a good day, but on us learning to pray the way that the New Testament teaches? What if God is always having a good day and sending us the answers to our prayers, only we don't receive them? Think about sports where one player throws a ball to another player and the receiving player just doesn't catch it! What if there are things in our lives that actually block us from receiving answers to our prayers?

What if God is always willing and ready to answer our prayers and the disconnect is us? What if there is a part in us somewhere deep inside that really just doesn't believe that God will answer our prayers? What if that disbelief is actually

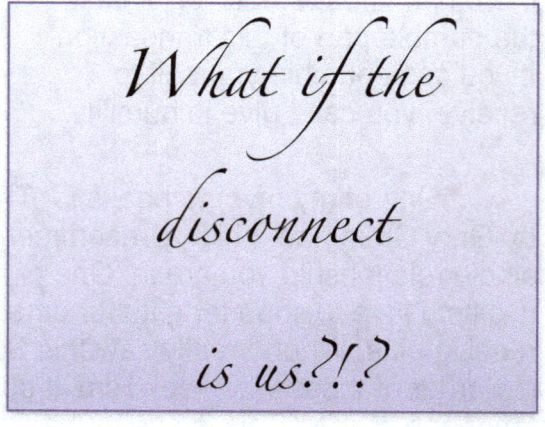

What if the disconnect is us?!?

keeping us from the reward of God? What if we can remove the blocks that hinder us in our prayer life and our walk with Jesus? Let's delve into this together and increase our faith for answered prayer!

Practicing His Presence

1) On a beautiful, clear night, stand outside and contemplate the immensity of our universe. Think about Jesus standing beside you and saying, "I made that! Isn't it marvelous?" Think about how much the One Who created everything you see in the night sky loves you! "When I consider Your heavens, the work of Your fingers, the moon and the stars, which You have ordained, What is man that You are mindful of him, and the son of man that You visit him?"   Psalm 8: 4 (NKJV)

2) Make a prayer list. You could dedicate a new journal to this or use a grocery list. The important thing is that you write down the things you are praying for.

3) Do you know your love language and the love language of those closest to you? If not, I recommend reading Dr. Chapman's book when you have time. There is even a quiz online that you and your friends and family can take.

4) Go over your prayer list with an honest and open heart. Do you really believe that the answers to those prayers are there? Mark the ones where you feel a "yeah, it's just a matter of time." Don't worry about the other ones. We'll talk about those later.

Notes

Chapter Two
The Faith of God

I was at my piano having fun playing, singing, and worshiping the Lord. The song I was enjoying was one my brother-in-law, Jon, had introduced to the family. In fact, it has become our Cox family anthem! He learned the song, The New Jerusalem, from it's composer, Alex Haley. The first verse begins with "It is done. You're the Alpha and Omega. It is done." On this particular day as I was singing these words, there was a deep knowing in my spirit. I felt like the Lord said, "This is My faith. It is already done." Needless to say, I became extremely undone, tears streaming down my face, as a glimmer of "It is done!" faith dawned on me.

Definition of Faith

Faith. I mean you can't have a book on faith for answered prayer without delving into the realm of faith! We'll explore both the biblical definition of faith and Webster's definition of faith. We'll look at the faith of God. Does He have faith? Can we emulate His faith? Think about that! What could you do if you had faith like God? We'll discuss the eternal present moment and what that has to do with our lives and faith. This chapter will lay a foundation on which we will build upon in subsequent chapters. We'll make sure our foundations of faith are firm!

The whole idea of faith seems like an enormous cloud of something that you cannot really grasp with your hands. It seems extremely ethereal and so mysterious that only a very few ever truly grab hold of genuine faith. But there is a Biblical concept of having the faith of God. Wait! What? God has faith? He's God! Isn't He faith itself? Let's get the Biblical definition of faith before we answer the question of whether or not God has faith. The subject and verb of this sentence, faith is, tells us that the author is about to give us the definition of faith. Faith is the substance.

"Now faith is the substance of things hoped for, the evidence of things not seen."
Hebrews 11:1 (NKJV)

A title deed. Confirmation. Reality. Assurance. Evidence. Faith comprehends as fact what is not yet experienced by our physical senses.

Webster's Dictionary defines *substance* as:
1. the real or essential part or element of anything; essence, reality, or basic matter
2. a) the physical matter of which a thing consists; material b) matter of a particular kind or chemical composition
3. a) solid quality; substantial character b) consistency; body
4. the real content, meaning or gist of something said or written
5. material possession; property; resources; wealth
6. something that has independent existence and is acted upon by cause or events.

So faith is the substance, physical matter or material, of what? Things hoped for.

Again let's look at Webster's dictionary. This time for the definition of *hope*.

1. a feeling that what is wanted will happen; desire accompanied by expectation
2. the thing that one has a hope for
3. a reason for hope
4. a person or thing on which one may base some hope
5. trust; reliance, to expect, look for.

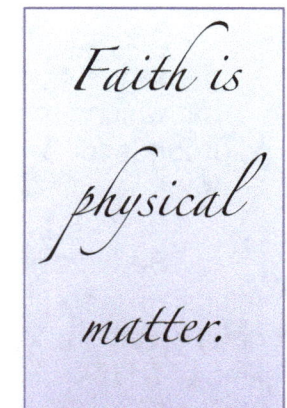

Don't we pray for the things we want? So faith is the physical matter or material of things that we feel can be had or that everything will work out for the best.

Webster's definition of faith is:
1. unquestioning belief that does not require proof or evidence
2. unquestioning belief in God, religious tenets
3. a religion or a system of religious beliefs
4. anything believed
5. complete trust, confidence, or reliance
6. allegiance to some person or thing; loyalty

Faith is the substance. Faith is the physical matter. Now take your physical matter of faith and hold it in your hands and look at it. Can you? I doubt it! But what is faith the substance of? Things hoped for; things that we feel can be had or that everything will work out for the best. I bet there is a thing or two or three in your life somewhere that you once hoped for and now you have it. There's the evidence of your faith!

The Scripture continues, "The evidence of things not seen."

"Now faith is the substance of things hoped for, the evidence of things not seen." Hebrews 11:1 (N

27

According to Webster's New World Dictionary, *evidence* is a noun.
1. that which tends to prove or disprove something;
2. grounds for belief;
3. proof.

So we can say that faith is the material matter of the things we want; the proof that they exist even though we can't see them! Wow! Wouldn't you just love to walk in that kind of faith?

God's Faith

Our original question was "does God have faith?" In order to discuss this, let's go to the beginning of all time and space as we know it — the first words of the Bible.

> "In the beginning God created the heavens and the earth. The earth was without form, and void; and darkness was on the face of the deep. And the Spirit of God was hovering over the face of the waters. Then God said, 'Let there be light'; and there was light."
>
> Genesis 1:1-3 (NKJV)

One could say that through His faith, God created the heavens and the earth. His faith was the material matter or substance of what He wanted. He wanted the heavens and the earth. He wanted humans created in His image! His faith was the proof that the heavens and the earth existed even though He could not see them yet. Through His faith the whole universe existed in Him before He spoke it into physical existence.

I love this verse in the book of Hebrews. I enjoy looking at this example of faith in various translations. Through faith, we can have an understanding of God's original creation!

> "By faith we understand that the worlds were framed by the word of God, so that the things which are seen were not made of things which are visible." Hebrews 11:3 (NKJV)

> "Faith empowers us to see that the universe was created and beautifully coordinated by the power of God's words! He spoke and the invisible realm gave birth to all that is seen."
> Hebrews 11:3 (TPT)

> "By faith we understand that the universe was formed at God's command, so that what is seen was not made out of what was visible." Hebrews 11:3 (NIV)

Have the Faith of God

Jesus taught a lot about faith. He told people who came to Him that it was *their faith* that saved them. It was *their faith* that healed them. It was *their faith* that made them whole. We'll discuss this more in a later chapter, but now let's look at Jesus' teaching His disciples to have the faith of God.

> "So Jesus answered and said to them, 'Have faith [*in/of*] God. For assuredly, I

say to you, whoever says to this mountain 'Be removed and be cast into the sea', and does not doubt in his heart, but believes that those things he says will be done, he will have whatever he says. Therefore I say to you, whatever things you ask when you pray, believe that you receive them, and you will have them.'"

Mark 11:22-24 (NKJV)(emphasis mine)

Peter Smythe explains the translation of "faith of God" as opposed to "faith in God" in great detail in his blog "The Faith of God (God-kind of Faith)". In this blog, he agrees with A.S. Worrell's translation and quotes him extensively. Here is a snippet of his thoughts on having the faith of God.

We possess the faith of God!

"From the research that I've done, I believe that A.S. Worrell puts it best: 'Have the faith of God; translators generally render this, 'Have faith in God'; but if this had been the thought, it would have been easy to have expressed it in the Greek. Faith originates with God; and those who have real faith have His faith; the same perhaps as 'the faith which is of the Son of God.'" Gal 2:20 Worrell, A.S., Worrell New Testament, note on Mark 11:22.

Mr Smythe continues, "Since Jesus did not say "faith in God", there is a good chance that He purposely meant "possess the faith of God." Mr. Smythe concludes his blog, "Indeed, it appears that only those who actually take Jesus at His word in Mark 11:22 as "[you] possess the faith of God" actually get to experience verses 23 and 24."

According to this teaching of Jesus, with the understanding of Mr. Worrell and Mr. Smythe, we have the faith of God! If we have the faith of God, then when we pray, believing and not doubting, that which we pray for will come to pass. If we have the faith of God that Jesus was talking about in Mark 11, mountain moving faith, what does that mean?

What does the faith of God look like?

How does this work and how can I learn to walk in it in my life? In the book of Revelation, the Apostle John saw the faith of God.

> "Now I saw a new heaven and a new earth, for the first heaven and the first earth had passed away. Also there was no more sea. "Then I, John, saw the holy city, New Jerusalem, coming down out of heaven from God, prepared as a bride adorned for her husband. And I heard a loud voice from heaven saying, 'Behold, the tabernacle of God is with men, and He will dwell with them, and they shall be His people. God Himself will be with them and be their God. And God will wipe away every tear from their eyes; there shall be no more death, nor sorrow, nor crying. There shall be no more pain, for the former things have passed away.' Then He who sat on the throne said, 'Behold, I make all things new.' And He said to me, 'Write, for these words are true and faithful.' And He said to me, 'It is done! I am the Alpha and the Omega, the Beginning and the End. I will give of the fountain of the water of life freely to him who thirsts.'" Revelation 21: 1-6 (NKJV)

Jesus was showing John the holy city, New Jerusalem. He was speaking as though it had already happened. And John was seeing it happen in a vision. Jesus said, "It is done!" by His faith! What John saw and left for us as the book of Revelation has not happened yet. New Jerusalem in not on the earth at this point in time, but God says, "It is done!" There is no question. There is no doubt. God's faith, although New Jerusalem has not yet descended, is so unwavering that to God it is already a done deal. There is no doubt. It is as though it's already happened.

This is the faith of God. Being so sure of a thing that you feel as though it already exists. That's what Jesus said in the mountain moving faith passage.

> "Whoever says… and does *not doubt* in his heart, but *believes* that those things he says will be done, he will have whatever he says."
>
> Mark 11: 23 (NKJV) (emphasis mine)

It's the "not doubting" and "believing that it's already a done deal" that's key here. This is how Jesus explains New Jerusalem to John. "It is done!" There is no doubt about its existence and coming to earth. "It is done!"

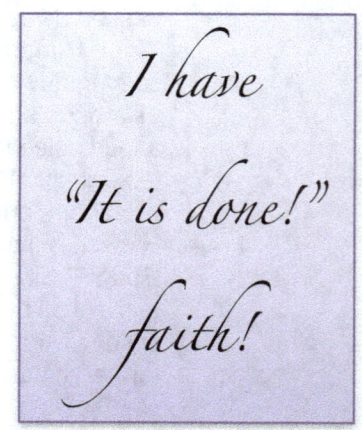

Jesus knew before He said, "Light Be!" that He would step into His creation and redeem it. He also knew that He would be victorious! There was no question. There was no doubt. He also knows that New Jerusalem will be reality.

"IT IS DONE!"
This is the Faith of God.

I was a new student at Regent University in Virginia Beach, Virginia. The University was only a few years old at the time and only had two departments; Education and Communications. I was a drama major. I had studied at the American Academy of Dramatic Arts and the Royal Academy of Dramatic Art. I was on a path to earn my Masters Degree in drama, or so I thought. The first week of classes, I mentioned this to an older student and she said, "No. Your degree will be in television production. You'll just take all the drama classes." I quickly said, "No. My degree will be in theatre."

I ended up meeting my future husband at Regent. We married and moved away before I completed my degree, but I had taken all the drama and production courses offered, so I was okay with leaving. Several years and four children later, one of our good friends from our Regent days was President of the University. A conversation with him got me on the path to completing my degree. Online course instruction was new at the time, but I was able to complete my degree! In May of 2000, I graduated from Regent University with a Masters of Communication in Theater Arts! That was the degree I knew in my heart of hearts that I would have.

For us, walking in our lives with the faith of God is a whole new ballgame. It's not wishy-washy thinking. It is knowing that something will be. Knowing that it already exists somewhere inside your being. Learning to walk in the faith of God is a key to having more faith for answered prayer! Paul gives us a glimpse of this new framework that Jesus instituted.

"For the law of the Spirit of life in Christ Jesus has made me free from the law of sin and death." Rom 8: 2 (NKJV)

We'll look more at this Scripture in a later chapter, but right now, we're going to learn one of the ways this whole new ballgame works.

This Eternal Present Moment

"…bringing every thought into captivity to the obedience of Christ…" 2 Cor 10:5b (NKJV)

Right now is where it all happens. Not in the past. Not in the future. You are here and now. You can't go back to the past and fix anything, and you can't fast forward into the future. Right now is your reality. All your memories of your life up to this moment were all created and lived in their present time. Our connect to life is now—This Eternal Present Moment. This moment, right now, is where we take all our thoughts captive. If our mind begins to wander into fear, we say, "No! I'm seated with Jesus in heavenly places!"

As followers of Jesus, we also live in the Kingdom of God. Jesus preached that the Kingdom of heaven and the Kingdom of God is at hand. He told a scribe in the Gospel of Mark that he, meaning the scribe, was not far from the kingdom. Scared the poor man so much that he and everyone else quit asking Jesus questions! I like to think that he became a follower of Jesus that day!

"The religious scholar replied, 'Yes, that's true, Teacher. You spoke beautifully when you said that God is one, and there is no one else besides him. And there is something more important to God than all the sacrifices and burnt offerings: it's the commandment to constantly love God with every passion of

34

your heart, with your every thought, and with all your strength—and to love your neighbor in the same way as you love yourself.' When Jesus noticed how thoughtfully and sincerely the man answered, he said to him, 'You're not far from the reality of God's kingdom.' After that, no one dared to question him again." Mark 12: 32-34 (TPT)

We are surrounded by this invisible Kingdom of God realm. I like to explain it as an overlay on our physical world. We can see our world. We can touch it, taste it, smell it, and hear it. Its existence is pretty obvious. It's also a reality from the Scriptures that it will be changed one day into a new earth.

The realm of the Kingdom of God is eternal. It is unchanging. It is the domain of Almighty God. His throne is there. It is God's dwelling place. And it's in this realm that we are seated with Him in heavenly places. It's an invisible overlay on our physical world.

In this very present, eternal moment that you are reading this page, I would like you to look around your environment and see the physical world that you live in. We walk here. Now imagine that the kingdom of heaven has enveloped your very real space. "On earth as it is in heaven." In 500 years, which of these realms will still exist? I can guarantee that the house I'm sitting in will not be around in 500 years! But the very fabric, this invisible overlay, of the kingdom of God, the kingdom of heaven, will definitely be around. Because it is the eternal kingdom!

Take a breath and sit with this for a moment. Which of these "realms" do you want to spend your effort on? We move in our earthly, physical realm with all our senses. We have to vacuum this realm over and over again!

We move in the realm of the kingdom of God with our spirit. Jesus told us to seek the kingdom of God, and all these things will be added to us. The Apostle Paul told us what the kingdom of God is made of in his letter to the Romans.

> "But seek first the kingdom of God and His righteousness, and all these things shall be added to you."
> Matthew 6:33 (NKJV)

> "So above all, constantly seek God's kingdom and his righteousness, then all these less important things will be given to you abundantly." Matthew 6:33 (TPT)

> "for the kingdom of God is not eating and drinking, but righteousness and peace and joy in the Holy Spirit."
> Romans 14:17 (NKJV)

> "For the kingdom of God is not a matter of rules about food and drink, but is in the realm of the Holy Spirit, filled with righteousness, peace, and joy."
> Romans 14:17 (TPT)

The secret of life is to enjoy this eternal, present moment — the moment of right now.

Doesn't the Kingdom of God sound like the fruit of the Spirit from Paul's letter to the Galatians? If we live with a consciousness of that eternal, invisible realm of the kingdom of God, then all the things of the physical realm fall into place. Practically speaking, while you are vacuuming this physical reality (or driving to work, or cooking dinner, or

36

cleaning the kitchen or bathroom) think about the things of God. Focus your mind on the good things of God. Focus your mind on the fruit of the Spirit. Learn to be the "connection" between the physical realm and the kingdom of God.

We are the connection between heaven and earth!

There is another side to this connection coin. In this eternal, present moment, this is where we connect with eternity. We are on the present moment "blip" of our earthly time line. The eternal realm where God dwells encompasses all of our universe and existence. So as you sit on your earthly couch, in your earthly timeline, in this eternal present moment, you have the ability to access the eternal realm!

Now is where we pray. Now is where we ask. Now is where we believe. Now is where we are seated with Jesus in the heavenly realm. So in this linear moment of our timeline, the time-less-ness of eternity is swirling all about us. Because we are created in God's image, eternal in spirit, we are also a part of this inexplicable swirling of eternity—in our present moment —while seated on our couches. This explains why sometimes we think only a few minutes have passed and we realize it's been hours. Or sometimes (usually when we're waiting on something or someone) it seems like it's been an hour and only a few minutes have passed.

Practicing His Presence

1) Take 5 minutes and sit and just think about God and His Kingdom. Think about Jesus sitting right beside you.

2) Look at your prayer list. Find one prayer where you know it's gonna happen, it just hasn't yet. An item on your list where you go, "Oh! That's the faith of God!" (If you don't find one, it will come, don't worry about it.)

3) Do this one by yourself, you will look and feel silly, but do it anyway! Faith is the substance. Looking at your prayer list, reach out with your hands and grab some of the substance of faith. It might be over your heart or it might be swirling about you in that unseen realm of God's kingdom. Take that faith in your hands and apply it to your prayer list as you pray.

Notes

Chapter Three
A Whole New Ballgame

God's realm, outside of our time and space, encompasses infinity beyond our universe. In the Old Testament, in Earth's realm, God relegated Himself to dwell in the Holy of Holies, between the cherubim. After Jesus' sacrifice on the cross and His resurrection, the Spirit of Almighty God chose to make us His dwelling place.

The Almighty God Who dwells outside of anything we've ever dreamed of knows and loves us! So much that He also dwells inside of us. The infinite, all-things-are-possible God is the treasure that we carry around in our finite, earthen vessels. We are in a whole, new ballgame! We are going to delve into what it means to be a follower of Jesus. What does it mean to be in Christ and for Christ to be in us? Can we truly have faith for impossible things? What about any desires of our hearts? Can we pray for these things, too?

Almighty God chose to live inside of us!

Emmanuel means God with us. God stepped into the world that He created in order to redeem it to Himself! That is an idea that seems so impossible, but He did it! God desired family. He wanted us to be with Him now and forever! I

40

asked the Lord once, "Why did You create the Universe? You had everything you needed. You were totally complete. Why?" I felt like He answered, "Because you weren't there."

Salvation

Salvation, right standing with God, is a status that only Jesus gives us. Because of the sacrifice of Jesus on the cross and His resurrection, our salvation is possible!

> "I will greatly rejoice in the Lord, My soul shall be joyful in my God, For He has clothed me with the garments of salvation, He has covered me with the robe of righteousness," Isaiah 61:10a (NKJV)

> "Therefore, if anyone is in Christ, he is a new creation; old things have passed away; behold, all things have become new." 2 Cor 5:17 (NKJV)

He has clothed us with His robe of righteousness. So if the changing of our very being through faith in Jesus is possible, something that is impossible for us, but possible with God, what is answered prayer compared to that? Living life with Jesus is the most important. Everything else is icing on the cake.

> "And they were greatly astonished, saying among themselves, 'Who then can be saved?' But Jesus looked at them and said, "With men it is impossible, but not with God; for with God all things are possible." Mark 10: 26-27 (NKJV)

These two Scriptures are talking about God reconciling those He created in His image to Himself. We cannot save ourselves. Only through the shed blood of Jesus and His resurrection can we be reconciled to Almighty God. Jesus went to great lengths to redeem us to Himself. That was His plan from creation. He wanted us as family, redeemed from the curse, and seated with Him. It stands to reason that He would also want to partner with us to answer more of our prayers. In the process of learning how to focus our asking in prayer, we are building our relationship with Almighty God! Salvation, new life in Jesus, is the ultimate answered prayer.

We have been set free from the curse!

I mentioned that my life changed on February 11, 1975. My brother and I were both students at Vanderbilt University. I had typed a paper for him titled "Marxism, Liberalism, and Christianity." Right in the middle of that paper two words stood out to me. Holy Ghost. They stuck with me for the duration of typing.

When my brother came to my dorm room to get his paper, I said, "Bill, what does the Holy Ghost do? I believe in Him. He's in the Apostles' Creed, but what does He do?" My brother took my Bible off my shelf and proceeded to show me the plan of salvation and the baptism of the Holy Spirit. I knew a more personal relationship with Jesus was what I had been longing for! I was a different person after that evening! Although I had been a believer in Jesus and Christianity that I had been taught in my church, I was now a follower of Jesus. I became an avid student of the Bible.

All things are possible

What is excluded from "all things"? Our rational, logical minds will try to tell us that He didn't actually mean "all things"! But think about it, God spoke everything into existence, so I really do believe that with God **all things** are possible. The catch is that little voice that whispers "but not for you". Why not? I think we're too busy explaining why we can't do something, or it's not for us, or…or…or… We should ask that little question more. Why not? WHY NOT?!? If you really think about that question seriously, those two words can be very intimidating!

"For with God nothing will be impossible."
Luke 1:37 (NKJV)

What's impossible with God? Nothing! Why do we think that God "can't" or "won't" do "that" for me? When that thought comes up, tell it to go away, then

God can do that for me!

pray for the "that" anyway! We have nothing to lose by praying for something that seems overwhelming to us, but we have the possibility of that prayer request coming to fruition! Why not pray for things that we think are

43

impossible? Perhaps it won't happen. But perhaps it will. Maybe. Sometimes. Wouldn't that be cool?

Is there anything that seems "impossible" in your life? Remember, it IS possible with God! When we learn to sit with Jesus in heavenly places and enter into His presence and His rest, something changes in our perspective. The "what-if's" begin to turn from the negatives to the positives. That's a wonderful life-view change!

Faith of God

And here we are back at the faith of God! If you will recall, having the faith of God is believing and acting like God does. When God says a thing will happen, it's as though it already has! There are no if's, and's, or but's about it. God has no doubt about the thing. In God's mind, there is already a new heaven and a new earth. No doubt whatsoever. We look at the outcome we would like and we think about the end—the thing we want to happen. God knows the end from the beginning. Jesus taught us how to have the faith of God. He said, "When you pray, believe you've already received, and you'll have whatever you ask for." Then rejoice in the Lord!

The impossible is possible in our lives!

Does this change the way we pray? Does it change our view of prayer? Does it make us bolder in our prayers? Maybe

44

asking for things that we think are quite impossible? Absolutely! It should! We can walk boldly into the very throne room of Almighty God, so we should have very bold prayers! He Who created the universe can do things we cannot imagine! Does this mean that we will have 100% of our prayers answered? Of course not! But what if? What if our prayers become more effective? Wouldn't that be awesome?

Delightful Prayer

"Delight yourself also in the Lord, and He shall give you the desires of your heart. Commit your way to the Lord, trust also in Him, and He shall bring it to pass."
Psalm 37:4-5 (NKJV)

What?!? God will give me the desires of my heart? Really? But He didn't really mean *MY* desires. That's only a kind of generic 'giving people the desires of their heart' scripture. Well, why wouldn't this particular scripture apply to us? It does! As we draw closer to the Lord, delighting in being with Him, it's His pleasure to give us the desires of our heart.

But He is wise in what He gives, because He won't give us what will harm us. What are the desires of your heart? What in your wildest imagination do you yearn for and yet don't believe that it is God's will? I had to ask the Lord to show me what the desires of my heart were because deep down, I really wasn't sure! I had not allowed myself to desire things because that seemed so selfish.

45

My husband and I went to a formal masquerade party a few years ago. About half the people had masks on and I was in that half. These were beautiful masks adorning the upper part of our faces around our eyes. I was talking with one of my neighbors who was also at the party but not wearing a mask. The thought crossed my mind that I should probably take my mask off. I nixed that thought because I was having so much fun dressed up in masquerade! I realized later that going to a "masquerade ball" had been a desire of my heart from childhood days. (Probably from reading Nancy Drew!) That made me wonder what other desires of my heart were hidden inside that I was not really aware of. I've asked the Lord to show me the desires of my heart!

So we pray! What do we pray for? Obviously, the everyday happenings, our families, people on our prayer list, and current events in both our neighborhoods and the world. But what about the desires of your heart? Do you even know what they are? Ask the Lord to reveal them to you! What would you love? When you sit with Jesus and just be silent with Him, does anything stir inside you?

What are the desires of your heart?

"Be anxious for nothing, but in everything by prayer and supplication with thanksgiving, let your requests be made known to God, and the peace of God, which surpasses all understanding, will guard your hearts and minds through Christ Jesus." Phil 4:6-7 (NKJV)

46

He Who created the universe can do things we cannot imagine! The images we're receiving from the James Webb Telescope show the amazing complexity and intricacies of our wonderful universe! And we are getting images from less than a pinpoint of the universe! The One Who created the universe and holds it together also knows every complexity and intricacy of your very life! He loves you so much and He only desires good for you.

> "Eye has not seen, ear has not heard, neither has entered the heart of man, the things that God has prepared for those who love Him."
> 1Cor 2:9 (NKJV)

Let's imagine BIG! Let's pray BOLDLY! Let us sit with Jesus in the heavenly places and ask, "What in the world, Daddy God, what would You have me ask for?"

> "Ask, and it will be given to you; seek, and you will find; knock, and it will be opened to you. For everyone who asks receives, and he who seeks finds, and to him who knocks it will be opened." Matt 7:7 (NKJV)

Practicing His Presence

1) Think about the day your life was changed by Jesus. If you don't have a specific date, think about Him in your life and all the good that has come from that relationship.

2) What do you think a "robe of righteousness" would look like? Try to imagine Jesus placing His righteousness around your shoulders like a robe.

3) Is there a prayer item on your list that seems impossible to you? Imagine that prayer item in your hands. Now imagine God's hands reaching down to you. Place that prayer request in His hands knowing that "with God all things are possible."

4) Ask God to show you the desires of your heart. Then as things come to you write them down.

Notes

Chapter Four
Mustard Seed Faith

Every human is born with faith. We were created in the image and likeness of God and He is the very essence of faith. We shall look into the fact that God has given to every single person more than enough faith! Isn't that awesome? We shall explore what mustard seed faith is and how much would be in the measure of faith that God has given to us. We will use that measure of faith to grow our very own forest of faith trees! Figuratively, that is! God rewards us for our faith. We saw that in the very first chapter. We will discuss how to believe and not doubt, and to carry that over into persistent prayer.

He rewards those who believe in Him.

Mustard Seed Parables

Jesus told two different parables about the mustard seed. In the first one, a whole field was planted in mustard seeds.

> "Another parable He put forth to them,
> saying: 'The kingdom of heaven is like a
> mustard seed, which a man took and sowed
> in his field, which indeed is the least of all the
> seeds; but when it is grown it is greater than
> the herbs and becomes a tree, so that the birds
> of the air come and nest in its branches.'"
> Matthew 13:21-21 (NKJV)

In this parable, Jesus is talking about a farmer growing a field of mustard seed trees so that the birds will have a place to nest. That is a beautiful picture of abundance! He also said that the kingdom of heaven is like this field of mustard seed trees. Everything we could ever want is right there! Wouldn't you love to have your slice of the "kingdom of heaven" in your life to look like this? I know I would!

In the second parable, Jesus teaches about the mustard seed in a little different way. He says that the size *of our faith* only needs to be as large as a mustard seed!

> "If you have faith as a mustard seed, you will
> say to this mountain 'Move from here to there,'
> and it will move; and nothing will be impossible
> for you.'" Matthew 17:20 (NKJV)

Think about these two scriptures together. Imagine that you have planted and tended a garden of mustard trees in your life, in your slice of the kingdom of heaven. Then at some point you need faith. You have a whole field of trees from which to harvest one tiny mustard seed. There would be millions of seeds in a field of trees, but according to Jesus, we only need ONE! Just one little glimmer of faith and that faith can grow as large as a tree!

Where does that original seed of faith come from? Where do we acquire mustard seeds in order to grow our forest of faith? The Apostle Paul mentions this in his letter to the Romans. He actually tells us where our original faith comes from!

"For I say, through the grace given to me, to everyone who is among you, not to think of himself more highly than he ought to think, but to think soberly, **as God has dealt to each one a measure of faith**."

Romans 12:3 (NKJV) (emphasis mine)

God is no respecter of persons and we are all equal in Christ Jesus. Everyone has the same amount of faith! Now a measure in New Testament times was about the size of a bushel basket. Imagine a bushel basket filled up with tiny seeds. That's a lot of "mustard seeds"! Maybe the farmer that Jesus talked about in His parable had a measure of mustard seeds to plant in his field!

We have a bushel basket full of mustard seeds of faith!

God has given us that original seed of faith. Since we are created in His image and faith emanates from Him we have His faith! God has given to every single human a whole bushel of faith ability. Imagine the forest of trees that a bushel of mustard seeds would grow; and then imagine all the mustard seeds contained in all the flowers on each of those mustard trees. Could we imply that God has actually given to us the ability to have *limitless* faith? I believe the answer is a resounding YES!

When my older son was about six years old, he and his sister had gotten into poison ivy. They were covered with it. My son also had a strange rash on his torso called a Christmas tree rash. To top that off, he had a cough, congestion, and low grade fever, probably from being outside in all the new spring growth of grasses, trees, and poison ivy. He was a miserable little fellow. I had slathered both of my kids with Calamine lotion before bed. I slept with my son in case he needed me during the night.

To get him to sleep, I sang a worship chorus and tickled his back. I kept repeating the chorus, and about the fourth or fifth time I felt this knowing inside me that went, "Yes! He is healed!" I was able to go to sleep peacefully and we both slept all night long.

The next morning, my son was noticeably happier. He felt better, but he was still pink and red. As I rubbed the sleep from my eyes and inspected him closer, the pink and red was the Calamine lotion. The poison ivy was gone. All but a half inch of the Christmas tree rash was gone. No fever. No congestion. Just a little bit of cough lingered. The really weird thing? His sister in the next room had no more poison ivy either!

I've had poison ivy a few times and it takes at least a couple of weeks to run its course and go away. This was less that 24 hours! I was only trying to keep my son comfortable from the itch and help him get to sleep. I was praying and worshiping the Lord. A little mustard seed of faith was there, but I must confess, it was very little. I was more concerned with his comfort. But a little mustard seed of faith and a miracle of healing occurred!

Believe and do not Doubt

Jesus continued teaching on mustard seed faith in Matthew 21 and Luke 17. In these verses, He told His disciples (and us) that their faith only has to be as big as a tiny, little mustard seed. We are going to look at those scriptures in a minute, but first, we're going to continue with the story that precedes our Matthew 17 verse.

Jesus and three of His disciples, Peter, James, and John, had been on the top of a mountain. Jesus had been transfigured before them. They saw Moses and Elijah talking with Jesus! Then God's voice spoke from the radiant cloud that surrounded them. This was a mind-blowing event and the disciples were terrified! On the way down the mountain, Jesus told them to not tell anyone about what they had seen until after His resurrection.

Have faith and do not doubt.

While the rest of the disciples waited for Jesus to return, a large crowd gathered. They wanted to see Jesus, too. When Jesus came down the mountain, a man approached Him and asked Him to heal his son.

"'I bought him to your followers, but they weren't able to heal him.' Jesus replied, 'Where is your faith? Can't you see how wayward and wrong this generation is?'"
Matthew 17: 16-17a (TPT)

54

Then Jesus healed the man's son and eventually He and His disciples move to another more private place. His disciples were used to asking Him to explain parables to them, but this time they asked Him why they couldn't heal the boy. Doesn't this sound like maybe they were used to healing others like Jesus did? Jesus was quick to point out that it was their lack of faith, their doubt, that kept them from healing the boy.

> "So Jesus said to them, "Because of your unbelief; for assuredly, I say to you, if you have faith as a mustard seed, you will say to this mountain, 'Move from here to there,' and it will move; and nothing will be impossible for you. However, this kind does not go out except by prayer and fasting.'"
> Matthew 17: 20-21 (NKJV)

There are a lot of books about fasting and a lot of studies have been done on the effects of fasting. I don't want to go into fasting here, but Jesus did make fasting and prayer a normal part of His everyday life. Many times the disciples would go and look for Him and He would be alone in prayer. He is our example, so prayer and fasting should be a part of our way of life, too. Fasting does not have to be a total giving up of food. We can fast a lot of things—dessert, meat, social media, television, you name it, it can be fasted. The important thing to remember while fasting is to spend that extra time with the Lord.

In these scriptures from Matthew 21 and Luke 17, Jesus continues teaching on faith. He enlarges the idea of having faith as the size of a mustard seed. In the first one, Jesus adds the phrase "do not doubt" when you have faith. In the second scripture, His disciples had specifically asked Him to increase their faith.

> "If you have faith and do not doubt, if you say

to this mountain, 'Be removed and cast into the sea,' it will be done." Matthew 21:21 (NKJV)

"And the apostles said to the Lord, 'Increase our faith.' So the Lord said, 'If you have faith as a mustard seed, you can say to this mulberry tree, 'Be pulled up by the roots and be planted in the sea,' and it would obey you.'" Luke 17:6 (NKJV)

In Matthew 21 above, Jesus said, "if you have faith and **do not doubt**," whatever you say will be done! Wow! We discussed this a bit in chapter two and having the faith of God, but let's delve into it further. I personally think that this next part - believing and not doubting - is a HUGE disconnect where answered prayer is concerned. Jesus coupled our faith with believing and not doubting over and over again.

"Therefore I say to you, whatever things you ask when you pray, believe that you receive them, and you will have them."
Mark 11:24 (NKJV)

"This is the reason I urge you to boldly believe for whatever you ask for in prayer - be convinced that you have received it and it will be yours."
Mark 11:24 (TPT)

Think about it. How many times have you prayed but you're really either on the fence about the prayer or you just really don't believe it will happen. Not that God *can't* do it or *won't* do it for you, but you just don't *believe* it will happen. James, the half-brother of Jesus, taught on this in his letter.

"Just make sure you ask empowered by confident faith without doubting that you will receive. For the ambivalent person believes one minute and doubts the next. Being undecided makes you become like the rough seas driven and tossed by the wind. You're up one minute and tossed down the next. When you are half-hearted and wavering it leaves you unstable. Can you really expect to receive anything from the Lord when you're in that condition?"

James 1:6-8 (TPT)

Anytime a doubt creeps into our thoughts, our faith begins to fade for whatever it is that we are praying for. Doubt is the enemy of faith. Jesus talked about a farmer who planted a whole field of mustard seeds and grew a field of trees. We only need one small seed in order to have great faith. AND, God has given to each and every one of us a whole bushel basket of mustard seeds of faith!

If you are a follower of Jesus, you probably prayed some sort of salvation prayer asking Jesus to come into your heart. Maybe you made a public confession of faith during confirmation. Whatever your case may be, you believed that Jesus was your Savior and you became His follower! Isn't that the most wonderful thing? This scripture in Romans is a very good example of believing when you pray. Followers of Jesus know that this prayer works! You ask and believe.

I am the way, the truth, and the life. No one comes to the Father except through Me.

~ Jesus

John 14:6 (NKJV)

57

"That if you confess with your mouth the Lord Jesus
and believe in your heart that God has raised Him
from the dead, you will be saved. For with the heart
one believes unto righteousness, and with
the mouth confession is made unto salvation."

Romans 10:9-10 (NKJV)

After your confession of faith, your Christian walk began. How marvelous that is! Whether we ever see Jesus with our mortal eyes or not, we know that He is with us — by faith. The very act of us stepping into our Christian faith is a perfect example of how Jesus taught His disciples to pray. "When you pray, believe you have already received, and you'll have whatever you ask for!" (my paraphrase) We ask Him to come into our lives. We believe He came into our lives. And He said He would never leave us nor forsake us!

Persistent Prayer

I love the way Dr. Brian Simmons explains patience in the footnotes of The Passion Translation. In his commentary on the fruit of the Spirit in Galatians 5:22, concerning the phrase "patience that endures", Dr. Simmons says, "The Greek word for patience is taken from a verb that means 'ever tapping' or 'never quitting'". I like this pro-active view on patience. In my mind, patience has always meant to sit quietly and wait like in a doctor's office or the Taco Bell line. But ever-tapping gives me a whole other view of patience, one to add to my sit quietly and wait view. (I usually take something with me to do or read if I know I'm going to be sitting quietly and waiting for any amount of time.)

58

According to Dr. Simmons, this same Greek ever-tapping verb is used in Luke 18:7. Jesus is telling His disciples a parable about being persistent in prayer. He talks about a widow who keeps going before an uncaring judge.

> "'Grant me justice and protect me against my oppressor!' He ignored her pleas for quite some time, but she kept asking."
> Luke 18:3b-4a TPT

Now I find it extremely odd that Jesus used a parable about a "judge, a think-skinned and godless man who had no fear of others' opinions" (Luke 18:2 TPT), basically a mean, cold, calculating judge, as an allegory to Father God. I believe that Jesus was trying to convey the idea that if a mean judge would finally give the widow what she asked for, how much more will God answer the persistent prayer of those He loves? According to Dr. Simmons, the same ever-tapping verb is used in verse 7.

> "don't you know that God, the true judge, will grant justice to all of His chosen ones who cry out to Him night and day? He will pour out his Spirit upon them." Luke 18:7 (TPT)

Dr. Simmons' commentary on this verse says,

Ever-tapping prayer

"Translated from the Aramaic text. The Greek text has an unusual verb that means "ever tapping" signifying one who keeps knocking on the door of heaven until he receives what he came for."

Ever-tapping. Do you keep ever-tapping in prayer? Most of my adult prayer life has been to pray

59

whatever I'm thinking at the moment, and that's okay. Spontaneous prayer is good! But an ever-tapping, persistent prayer strategy needs a little more structure. Prayer journals or just a good prayer list would work well for this. You make a specific list of the things you're praying for. Make sure they fall in line with Jesus' injunction on prayer.

> "Therefore I say to you, whatever things you ask when you pray, believe that you receive them, and you will have them."
> Mark 11:24 (NKJV)

Then keep the list with you and pray over it several times a day—ever-tapping prayer. Remember, Jesus said all we needed was faith the size of a mustard seed and we have a whole bushel basket full of faith! Be patient with ever-tapping prayer and see what unfolds in your life.

Practicing His Presence

1) Look up a picture or go get a packet of mustard seeds. Remember our earlier practice of holding this invisible substance of faith in our hands? How many mustard seeds would it take to fill your hands? Think about how many mustard seeds would be in a bushel basket!

2) Read about the time it takes for a mustard seed to germinate and grow into a flowering plant. Sometimes our prayers are answered quickly and sometimes it just takes time.

3) If you are so inclined, plant of few mustard seeds and what them grow!

4) Look at your prayer list. Are there items on your list that you have doubts about? If so, find your level of faith for that item and pray for that. By doing this, you will eventually move yourself to the level of faith that you have no doubt about this prayer.

Notes

Chapter 5

Increase Your Faith

I'm so glad you are now cultivating a lifestyle of faith! In this chapter, we are going to go deeper into this idea of faith. We are going to explore ways to put muscle to our faith so that we can use our faith more efficiently. We are going to look at numerous scriptures where Jesus actually told people that the answer they received from Him was because of their faith! We are going to talk about living life in the Spirit of God. We are going to find things we do that will either help or hinder our faith. We are going to look at two things concerning faith that astonished Jesus. I would like to astonish Jesus with my faith, wouldn't you? We'll pull all of this together and maybe, just maybe, we'll be able to go into our forest of faith and be amazing with and to our Lord!

> *"If you want faith for answered prayer, you must increase your faith."*

This seems like a silly statement. It should go without saying, but I believe this is a biggie for us. Somehow we tend to think we either have faith or we don't. Is faith like a muscle that we can exercise and make stronger? I do believe we can make our faith stronger, but how do we go about doing that? We've actually begun this with our mustard seed practices! Let's add to this and help them grow from seeds to seedlings and then a whole forest!

Acts of Faith

An act of faith means that you begin working toward something when you can't see the end result. Don't we do this all the time in our everyday ordinary lives? For instance, dinner won't get cooked until someone pulls something out of the refrigerator. The end product, dinner on the table, does not happen until we create it. We do similar things all throughout each day.

Let's take this idea and move it into the realm of our prayer life. Like dinner on the table, the answers to our prayers are not sitting right in front of us. We can see them in our mind's eye, otherwise we wouldn't be praying for them. Can we increase our faith for these prayers by acting on our faith? James, the half brother of Jesus, made an interesting correlation between faith and works.

> "But someone might object and say, 'One person has faith and another person has works.' Go ahead then and prove to me that you have faith without works and I will show you faith by my works as proof that I believe." James 2:18 (TPT)

Now James is not talking about working for our salvation. No. Salvation is a free gift to those created in God's image. The example that James used in the verses preceding verse 18 was someone who blessed fellow believers but did nothing to help alleviate their suffering. Their fellow believers were hungry and cold, but the person of faith sent them away with a blessing not with anything that would help them. James is saying that if the person had clothed and fed his brothers and sisters in Christ, he would have demonstrated his faith with his works.

So can we also act on our faith concerning the things that we are praying about? Absolutely! For instance, let's say you are praying for more income to help you make it through the end of the month with a bit of money left over. What might you do as an act of your faith to help in this situation?

There was a time when my children were little and we were going through a lot of milk. I purchased a box of dry milk and I cut our gallon of whole milk with a thinner mix of dry milk. Honestly, when it was poured over cereal, no one could tell the difference! But this saved a few dollars every month. I also bought the larger bags of generic cereal which added to our savings. This was an act of faith to have more money at the end of the month by saving dollars where I could during the month. And I prayed and asked the Lord for wisdom to make more money. He saw us through then and He still does now! He is ever faithful!

Recently, as an act of faith, I enrolled in a writing challenge course to help me finish the work on this manuscript. One of the first things I was to do was to find three intercessors to pray for me during this time of writing. One of my friends said, "Sure! But I need to know more." So I proceeded to text her the particulars of the course and that I needed a kick in the pants and accountability. She said, "That's great, but what is the theme of your book?" So I gave her my working title "Faith for Answered Prayer." She texted back, "Thanks for telling me about the book. I will pray. Which seems kind of funny since the book is about having faith in prayer!"

God's Word Stands!

God's word does not return to Him void, but it prospers in the thing for which He sent it.

(IS 55:11)

My paraphrase

So far, we've explored the Faith of God and what that means for us to have God's faith. God knows the end from the beginning, so when He says something, it's already a done deal. Period. Whether it's come to pass yet or not.

> "Remember the former things of old, For I am God, and there is no other; I am God, and there is none like Me, Declaring the end from the beginning, And from ancient times things that are not yet done, Saying, 'My counsel shall stand, and I will do all My pleasure,'" Isaiah 46:9-10 (NKJV)

God is not concerned whether or not New Jerusalem will be ready at the appointed time. It will be. There is no question about it. He is outside of our time frame and somehow, in His God-ness, it is already done.

> "For as the rain comes down, and the snow from heaven, And do not return there, But water the earth, And make it bring forth and bud, That it may

66

give seed to the sower and bread to the eater,
So shall My word be that goes forth from My
mouth; It shall not return to Me void, But it shall
accomplish what I please, and it shall prosper
in the thing for which I sent it." Isaiah 55: 10-11 (NKJV)

God's eternal realm in which He lives encompasses our time and space universe. There's an idea that will blow your mind if you think about it too long! God exists outside of our time and space! He is the One Who was, Who is, and Who is to come. He is from everlasting to everlasting. He has no beginning and He has no ending. He always was and He always will be! From His vantage point, there is not a bit of doubt. None whatsoever. Not even a hint. Sit with Him in the heavenly places on a regular basis. Just be with Him and contemplate His creation. Keep doing this until you are completely trusting in Him. Then keep sitting with Him because that is where you belong! God raised you up and placed you there!

Let's look again at Jesus' words from Mark 11. This time, keep in mind the idea of the faith of God. The things that you're praying for, do you believe that you've already received them even though they haven't happened yet? Read this verse with the idea of your faith being a physical substance.

"Therefore I say to you, whatever things you
ask when you pray, believe that you receive
them, and you will have them." Mark 11:24 (NKJV)

Do you know that you know that you know that that thing you're praying for is already in existence in God's infinite abundance? Do you really believe deep down in your being that you will have what you are asking for? Or are you hoping (in a wishing sort of way) that maybe it might happen? There is NO DOUBT with Almighty God that the end of Revelation will turn out just as John saw it! Can you get that kind of God faith with your prayer list?

67

Many times in my life, I've just known in my gut that something I wanted would come to fruition. I was at a crossroads (figuratively speaking) in my early twenties. I had attended the American Academy of Dramatic Arts and I was about to participate in a Shakespeare workshop at the Royal Academy of Dramatic Art in London. (Oh gosh! That was fun!) But I had no idea what I was going to do when I returned.

Believe that your prayer is already answered in the eternal realm.

Randomly at church one Sunday morning, a lady gave me a brochure about the drama department at Regent University. This was early summer and their deadline for fall classes had already passed. Something inside me said, "This is it! This is where I'm going!" Regent was founded by Pat Robertson of CBN and the 700 Club. For me, the thought of studying drama from a Christian perspective with fellow believers was very exciting.

I made an appointment with the Dean of Admissions and drove from Nashville to Virginia Beach for a long weekend. My brother, the daughter of the lady who gave me the brochure, and the daughter's best friend all went with me. We had a wonderful time!

During my appointment, the Dean looked over all my records from Vanderbilt and my GSAT scores. I had taken the GSAT while at Vanderbilt just on a whim, because I had no desire to ever go back to school again! And here I was sitting across the desk of the Dean of Admissions of Regent

University. After our thirty minute interview, Dean Gyertson stood up, shook my hand, and said, "Welcome to Regent." I breathed a sigh of relief. I was also struck with an awe because that thing that I believed would happen actually did happen!

My Faith

We've seen the importance of physically asking Father God for our specific prayer requests. James tells us to ask and to ask with right motives. God knows everything you need and He knows the thoughts and intents of your heart. You can trust God to ask Him the things you need and desire!

> "And all the time you don't obtain what you want because you won't ask God for it!" James 4:2b (TPT)

This makes me want to ask a whole lot more! We've talked about the analogy of faith like a mustard seed and if we plant our bushel full of faith seeds, we just may end up with limitless faith! And we've also explored the idea of believing that you've already received the answer to your prayer when you ask it.

Now we are going to look at a few scriptures and then discuss them as a whole. As you read these scriptures, try to place yourself in the shoes of the person who is approaching

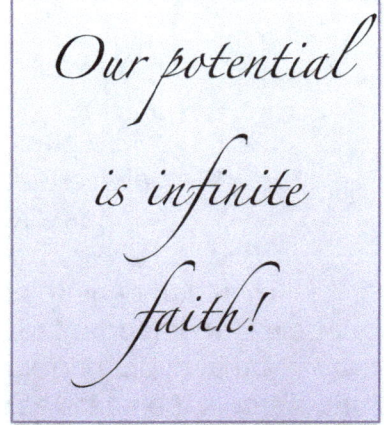

Our potential is infinite faith!

Jesus and asking for something.

"O woman, great is your faith! Let it be to you as you desire." Matthew 15:28 (NKJV)

"Daughter, your faith has made you well. Go in peace, and be healed of your affliction." Mark 5:34 (NKJV)

"Then Jesus said to him, 'Go your way; your faith has made you well.'" Mark 10:32 (NKJV)

(Jesus said to the Samaritan leper,) "Arise, go your way. Your faith has made you well." Luke 17:19 (NKJV)

"Receive your sight; your faith has made you well." Luke 18:42 (NKJV)

In these scriptures on the faith of the person, Jesus is saying that the healing of all these particular people is because of *their faith;* as their faith—so is their healing. This is kind of a scary topic. What if the answers to all my praying hinges on my faith that it will be done? Again, it's not the issue of "can God do something". Of course He can! The nagging thought in the back of our heads is "will God do it— *for me*?"

We walk in the faith of God.
We ask.
We plant a garden of faith.
We believe that what we ask for in faith
has already been done.

This then begs the question: Is our faith, our asking, our belief, so important to Almighty God that answers to prayer are in direct correlation to our faith? If so, then our hearts' cry is the same as that of the father whose son

70

needed healing after Jesus returned from the Mount of Transfiguration.

> "Jesus said to him, 'If you can believe, all things are possible to him who believes.' Immediately the father of the child cried out and said with tears, 'Lord, I believe; help my unbelief!'" Mark 9:23-24 (NKJV)

I do want to make a disclaimer here. I don't want to create any place of doubt for your desires in prayer. However, at the time of this writing, I have two grandsons ages 3 and 4 and their biggest desire right now is to have a real, working excavator that they can play with. That just ain't gonna happen! Sit with the Lord and ask for wisdom concerning your desires and prayers. Some of the things that we are asking for could put us in harm's way as much as toddlers playing with real excavators. Trust the Lord. Remember God knows both the beginning and the ending.

May your prayer be answered according to your faith.

So in this discussion, when Jesus says your faith, we want to look at it now as our faith. If Jesus were to say to me, as He did to the woman from Canaan In Matthew 15: 28, "O woman, great is your faith! Let it be to you as you desire," I might answer Him, "**My** faith? **Mine**?!? Oh my Lord Jesus! Help my faith!!!" Let's look at the whole story of the Canaanite woman.

"Then Jesus went out from there and departed
to the region of Tyre and Sidon. And behold,
a woman of Canaan came from that region
and cried out to Him, saying, 'Have mercy on
me, O Lord, Son of David! My daughter is
severely demon-possessed.' But He answered
her not a word. And His disciples came and
urged Him, saying, 'Send her away, for she
cries out after us.' But He answered and said,
'I was not sent except to the lost sheep of
the house of Israel.' Then she came and
worshiped Him saying, 'Lord, help me!' But
He answered and said, 'It is not good to take
the children's bread and throw it to the little
dogs.' And she said, 'Yes, Lord, yet even the
little dogs eat the crumbs which fall from their
masters' table.' Then Jesus answered and
said to her, 'O woman, great is your faith! Let
it be to you as you desire.' And her daughter
was healed from that very hour."

Matthew 15: 21-28 (NKJV)

Wait! Did I read that correctly? Did Jesus really call
her a dog? Remember, as Messiah (and this Canaanite
woman used a Messianic term when she addressed Jesus
as "Son of David"), Jesus came to Israel to fulfill all the
prophecies concerning Him. The Israelites would not even
eat with Gentiles. But we know Jesus. This seems
uncharacteristic of Him, even toward a Canaanite woman.
He knows everything and I think He knew what it would take
to get this woman to the height of her faith.

Her daughter had a bad problem—demon-
possession. I'm sure she had heard stories about Jesus and
she knew He was her only hope for her daughter. She asked
and was ignored. Her love for her daughter pushed her to
ask again. This Canaanite woman kept asking. She was
using ever-tapping prayer! She kept following Jesus and His
disciples. They urge Him to do something; to send her away.

She takes advantage of the lull in motion (my theory) and places herself right in front of Jesus and knelt before Him.

She worshiped Him. Something inside of her knew that He was Messiah and that He could heal her daughter. And He calls her a dog. She doesn't miss a beat, "Even the dogs eat the crumbs that fall from their master's table." She came to Jesus desperate. Her Mama Bear instincts came out and made her bold in her approach of Him. Her answer moved Him to grant her request—*because of her great faith!*

We see the Canaanite woman go from desperate to bold in her asking Jesus for a miracle of healing. Don't you know with every step her faith increased? So the question that consumes us now is, "How do we increase our faith?" The tiny letter of Jude, another half brother of Jesus, is a good place to start.

> "But you, beloved, *building yourselves up on your most holy faith*, praying in the Holy Spirit, keep yourselves in the love of God, looking for the mercy of our Lord Jesus Christ unto eternal life." Jude 20 (NKJV) (emphasis mine)

This verse mentions three things that build up our faith; praying in the Holy Spirit, stay in the love of God, and look for the mercy of our Lord Jesus Christ. We shall look at each of these individually.

Praying in the Holy Spirit

If you are a believer in Jesus, the Christ, and He has come to make His home inside of you, then you are filled with the Holy Spirit of Almighty God. This is not a discussion

73

about the baptism of the Holy Spirit with the evidence of speaking in tongues that is mentioned in Acts, chapter 2, and other places. I do heartily agree with that and I believe it is for all followers of Jesus, but that's not what we are talking about here. Certainly, if you do pray in tongues, Jude 20 also includes that aspect of prayer, but it is not exclusive to it. The 8th chapter of Romans is an excellent overview of the Spirit-filled life.

"Likewise the Spirit also helps in our weaknesses. For we do not know what we should pray for as we ought, but the Spirit Himself makes intercession for us with groanings which cannot be uttered. Now He who searches the hearts know what the mind of the Spirit is, because He makes intercession for the saints according to the will of God." Romans 8: 26-27 (NKJV)

We've been talking about increasing our faith for answered prayer and shall continue to do so. I mean, that's what we all want, right? To see more affirmative answers to the things we pray. This idea of praying in the Holy Spirit, includes praying our list of prayer items, but it goes even further. It goes into that realm of praying for people and things when we don't even know how to pray. The words don't come. We feel stymied.

It's sitting with the Lord in holy silence while we think about the things we have no words for. We feel within our spirit the things and people we would like the Lord to work in and we lay all that out before the Lord. He knows all things and He desires the best for all humanity. As we sit with the Lord, praying, we try to see the big picture of what we are asking for. See it completed in our imagination like John saw New Jerusalem descending in his vision. Then when we see our desired answer to prayer, we say, "Yes, Lord, that is my desire. May it be so."

Keep yourselves in the love of God

Stay in **LOVE. Period.** When Jesus was asked what the greatest commandment was, He talked about loving God with everything that's in us. Then He added a second commandment equal to the first. Loving all those created in His image..

> "Then one of them, a lawyer, asked Him a question, testing Him and saying, 'Teacher, which is the great commandment in the law?' Jesus said to him, 'You shall love the Lord your God with all your heart, with all your soul, and with all your mind.' This is the first and great commandment. And the second is like it: 'You shall love your neighbor as yourself. On these two commandments hang all the Law and the Prophets.'" Matthew 22: 36-40 (NKJV)

ALL the Law and the Prophets hang on these two commandments! The whole Old Testament hangs on these two commandments! We are to love the Lord our God with all that is in us. We are to love our neighbor as we love ourselves.

Love

What did Jesus do? He gave us a NEW testament! All because God so *loved* the world that He created! All because God so *loved* the ones that He created in His image! Jesus came into the world and died because HE loved us so much! We are to walk in that kind love!

Well, let's look at Jesus' second greatest commandment. "You shall love your neighbor as you love yourself." Jesus was quoting a law from Leviticus concerning the stranger who lived among the children of Israel.

> "The stranger who dwells among you shall be to you as one born among you, and you shall love him as yourself; for you were strangers in the land of Egypt: I am the Lord your God." Lev 19:34 (NKJV)

> "You shall love your neighbor as yourself."
> Matthew 22: 39 (NKJV)

Many times the second half of this verse is left off so we end up with loving our neighbor. But according to the second half of this verse, if I don't love myself, I cannot love my neighbor. Do you truly love yourself or are you constantly berating yourself over something? You can't give what you don't have. Begin by truly loving yourself, genuinely honoring and respecting yourself.

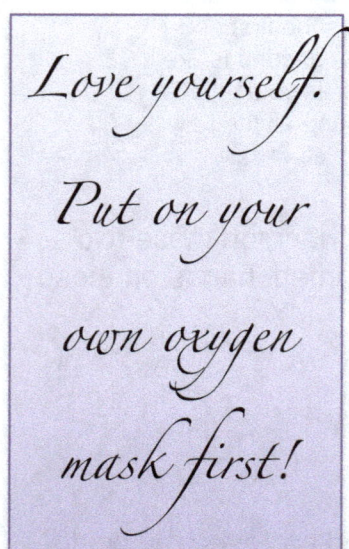

Love yourself.

Put on your

own oxygen

mask first!

What is your inner chatter toward yourself? What do you really think when you look at yourself in the mirror? Do you kick yourself for something you said in conversation and later you think it was stupid? Do you say to yourself, silently or out loud, things you would never say to someone else? You are the beloved of Jesus. See yourself and love yourself as Jesus loves you.

1 Corinthians 13 is called the love chapter because Paul talks about the importance of believers living their lives in love. The beginning of the chapter is saying that we can build great empires and do amazing works for the Lord, but if love is not part of the process, it's not worth anything. God is love and we are to allow His love to shine through us.

> "If I were to speak with eloquence in earth's many languages, and in the heavenly tongues of angels, yet I didn't express myself with love, my words would be reduced to the hollow sound of nothing more than a clanging cymbal. And if I were to have the gift of prophecy with a profound understanding of God's hidden secrets, and if I possessed unending supernatural knowledge, and if I had the greatest gift of faith that could move mountains, but have never learned to love, then I am nothing."
>
> 1 Corinthians 13: 1-2 (TPT)

Interesting. We've discussed mountain moving faith quite a bit! According to this scripture, if we do end up with faith to have all our prayers answered but we don't have love, we really don't have anything. A genuine smile and kind word to a cashier means more in God's economy than a million dollar business run by a tyrant who does not care about his or her employees. Now each employee has the freedom to choose to live in love under said tyrant! Make sure love is walked out in your life!

Walk in love.

I don't think a discussion about staying in love, period, is complete without touching upon the concept of forgiveness. Because unforgiveness is not walking in love! Jesus makes a really odd statement in Matthew concerning forgiveness.

> "For if you forgive men their trespasses,
> your heavenly Father will also forgive you.
> But if you do not forgive men their trespasses,
> neither will your Father forgive your
> trespasses." Matthew 6:14-15 (NKJV)

But aren't our sins forgiven by the finished work of Jesus on the cross? Don't we live life with Him in His resurrection? Yes and absolutely! I believe Jesus talked about forgiving others (or not) in such a weird, strict way because unforgiveness and bitterness wreaks so much havoc in our lives that it is not worth having. If you can't forgive someone for something they did to you, that hurt, anger, and bitterness will continue to eat you up on the inside.

Most of the time, the unforgiveness inside of you usually does not hurt the other person. In most cases, they don't even know, or if they do, they don't care that you haven't forgiven them. Usually they feel they've done nothing to be forgiven for! Unforgiveness and bitterness only harm the person who continues to harbor it in their hearts. If your heart is full of unforgiveness and bitterness, there's not a lot of room for love in it. The best thing to do in a situation like this —no matter what the infraction was or by whom—is to forgive and rid yourself of those negative emotions.

Forgive.

This is so easy to say, but so hard to do. It's a little bit here and a little bit there. Every time unforgiveness rears its ugly head, you speak peace over that person and over yourself. You don't ever have to tell them or see them again, but you do need to rid yourself of those emotions. They are not worth carrying around.

Mercy

Our society seems to be increasingly harsh, selfish, and judgmental. You don't have to look too long on social media to find complaints and complainers. We, as believers, are in this world but not of this world. We should be the cross-culture ones who show mercy. Instead of seeing the bad in circumstances and people, look for mercy. Look for the positive instead of the negative. Look for times and areas where you can encourage others and show kindness.

> "For judgment is without mercy to the one who has shown no mercy. Mercy triumphs over judgment." James 2:13 (NKJV)

Mercy is a noun; a person, place, or thing. In this particular situation, mercy is a thing. Mercy, like faith, is not a physical object that one can pick up, but it is something you can give to others. According to Webster's dictionary, mercy is "refraining from harming or punishing offenders, enemies, persons in one's power." In other words it is compassion toward someone that you could really hurt.

Bless those who treat you badly.

79

In our everyday lives this would correlate to looking for the good in people and situations instead of being critical and picking things to pieces. It is looking for the silver lining in every cloud. It's looking for the positive instead of the negative. It's being pro-active about giving compliments to others, even if it's only silently to yourself. Find something good that you can say or think about the other person. Look for the mercy instead of the judgement. One of the ways that Jesus taught about mercy can be found in the golden rule.

> "In everything you do, be careful to treat others in the same way you'd want them to treat you, for that is the essence of all the teachings of the Law and the prophets."
> Matthew 7:12 (TPT)

So in summing up the three things that Jude tells us to do to build up our faith, it all boils down to relationship. When you're with someone you trust, whose company you enjoy, you can allow cares and worries to fade into the background for the time being. When we spend time in our relationship with Jesus, reading His Word, praying, walking in the love of God, looking through His eyes, our faith naturally increases. Our most holy faith grows.

Prayer

Love

Mercy

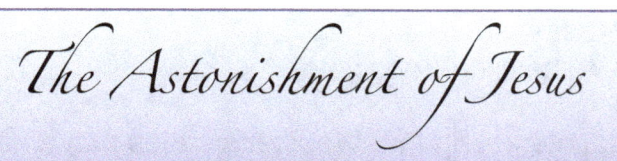

The Astonishment of Jesus

Jesus marveled at, was astonished by, two things; a Roman Centurion and the people of His hometown of Nazareth. We are going to look at Webster's definition of a few words to try to capture Jesus' emotions surrounding these two encounters. The first word is marvel. Jesus marveled. What does this mean?

Marvel
1. a wonderful or astonishing thing;
2. prodigy or miracle;
3. to be filled with admiring surprise;
4. be amazed;
5. to wonder at or about
   Isn't it a marvelous word?

According to this definition, the word marvel seems to be a very positive, surprised emotion, but we know that in Nazareth, Jesus' reaction was not in the affirmative. So let's dig a little more. We'll now look at Webster's definition of the second word that describes Jesus' emotions.

Astonish
1. to fill with sudden wonder or great surprise;
2. amaze

Again, this definition seems very positive, yet we all know that we can shake our heads in astonishment because of negative circumstances. Let's look at one more word that both of these definitions mention—amaze.

Amaze
1. to fill with great surprise or sudden wonder;

2. astonish

3. to bewilder (obsolete)

It's interesting that Webster's states that amazement in the obsolete means bewilderment. So now we have two marvelous words, marvel and astonish, that are amazing. They can be used for both positive and negative circumstances. Let's look at the two circumstances in which Jesus marveled.

The Roman Centurion who understood authority, and had no doubt that Jesus had the authority to heal, was one of them. Remember that Roman Centurions were officers in the Roman Army. They were an occupying force in Israel. They were hated. The soldiers looked down upon Israel and everything it stood for. The Roman Emperor was their god. They were the victorious force. They usurped their authority over Israeli citizens every time they could. Yet, this Centurion came to Jesus on behalf of one he loved and wanted healed. All Jesus had to do was say the word and his servant would be healed. Jesus called this "great faith."

> "Therefore I did not even think myself
> worthy to come to You. But say the word,
> and my servant will be healed. For I also
> am a man placed under authority, having
> soldiers under me. And I say to one, 'Go,'
> and he goes; and to another, 'Come,' and
> he comes; and to my servant, 'Do this,' and
> he does it." When Jesus heard these things,
> He marveled at him, and turned around and
> said to the crowd that followed Him, "I say to you,
> I have not found such great faith, not even in
> Israel!" Luke 7:7-9 (NKJV)

Two things are going on in this story. The Centurion understood authority, he was a man of authority and he knew it. When he told someone to do something, he knew it would get done. In the Roman army there were dire consequences

Jesus marveled and was amazed at the Roman Centurion's faith!

to the soldier who disobeyed orders. The Centurion had authority over his soldiers and he knew it.

He also saw the authority that Jesus walked in. As a soldier of authority, he recognized authority when he saw it. He saw it in Jesus. He didn't consider it faith that Jesus had. He saw that Jesus had authority. He just knew if Jesus said a word, it would happen. Jesus called this man's understanding of authority "faith". In fact, Jesus marveled at the Roman soldier's faith! Jesus said he had not found such great faith even in Israel! Can you imagine some of the reactions of the crowd around Jesus when He said this?

There was another place that Jesus marveled at their faith—or the lack of it. The people of his hometown of Nazareth had watched Jesus grow up. They knew He was the son of Joseph and Mary. They also knew the rumors about His birth and was the carpenter really the father? When He spoke in their synagogue, they could not receive the Word He taught because they could not look past His life among them. They could only see a disgraced, carpenter's son. The Word says that He could do no mighty works there because of their lack of faith.

> "Now He could do no mighty work there, except that He laid His hands on a few sick people and healed them. And He marveled because of their unbelief." Mark 6:5-6 (NKJV)

Think about this. Jesus could do NO MIGHTY WORK there because of their unbelief! Doesn't this scripture sound like He was bewildered at their unbelief?

There is another scripture found in the book of Hebrews that talks about the children of Israel walking in unbelief and that is why they were unable to enter into the promised land. This was after the twelve spies were sent in to scout the land and only Joshua and Caleb believed that the Lord had given the land to them. The other spies brought a bad report and the congregation listened to them instead. Because of this they wandered around the wilderness for forty years.

Unbelief blocks faith

"The same people who were delivered from bondage and brought out of Egypt by Moses, were the ones who heard and still rebelled. They grieved God for forty years by sinning in their unbelief, until they dropped dead in the desert. So God swore an oath that they would never enter into his calming place of rest all because they disobeyed him. It is clear that they could not enter into their inheritance because they wrapped their hearts in unbelief."
Hebrews 3: 16-19 (TPT)

They wrapped their hearts in unbelief. Think about that for a minute. The Hebrew children in the wilderness chose to listen to the bad report of the ten spies instead of the good report of Joshua and Caleb. The people of Nazareth could not see beyond Someone Who had grown up in their midst. They also wrapped their hearts in unbelief. Let's take another look at our scripture in Mark concerning Jesus' words on prayer.

"Whatever things you ask when you pray, believe that you receive them and you will have them." Mark 11:24 (NKJV)

If we turn this verse inside out so to speak and look at it in the negative, we will get a deeper understanding of what Jesus is saying. Sometimes if we look at the opposite of what the scripture says, it gives more clarity on its true meaning.

"When you pray, if you don't believe you will get your prayers answered, you will not have what you ask for!"

If our hearts are wrapped in unbelief, we will also experience no mighty work like the people of Nazareth! Oh my! If I want my prayers to be answered, I do need to work on believing that I receive them and not doubt. May it never be said of us that we wrapped our hearts in unbelief!

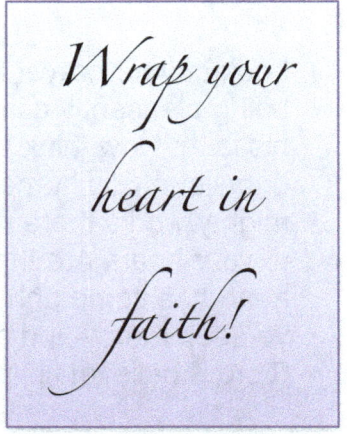

There is an authority that we walk in as followers of Jesus. The Roman Centurion understood the authority that he walked under, and he saw that Jesus walked under authority. But the authority that Jesus walked under was hindered by the people of His hometown who did not believe in Him. They could not see His authority. As followers of Jesus, we sit with Him in heavenly places, and we have His perspective on our lives. We learn to walk in His authority. It begins with learning to believe that you receive the things that you pray for when you pray for them.

Practicing His Presence

1) Is there any where in your life where you could do an act of faith? Look at your prayer list. Is there any step you could take that might move you toward the answer?

2) Memorize Mark 11: 24.

3) Think about the Canaanite woman. In what way do you identify with her?

4) Using the Jude 20 verse, begin a daily plan to build yourself up in your most holy faith. Be intentional to pray in the Spirit, walk in love, show mercy to yourself and others.

5) Look at your prayer list with honesty. Think about Jesus being pleasantly astonished at the Roman Centurion and his faith. Now think about Jesus being bewildered by the unbelief of His hometown and how He couldn't do many mighty works there. Go through your prayer list and listen to your heart. Are there any items there that you feel your heart has some unbelief wrapped around it? Give yourself mercy and ask the Lord to help your unbelief. "Lord, I believe! Help my unbelief!"

Notes

In order to ask for specific things in our prayers, we must first know what we want to ask for. This is not the "Lord,

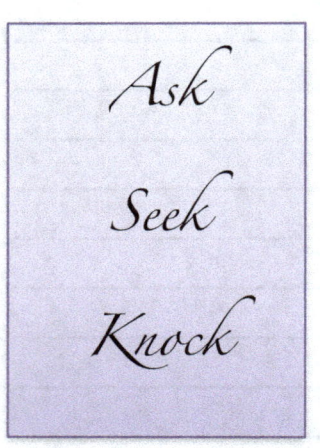

whatever You want, that's what I want" prayer. If you've come this far with me in this book, I'm sure that every fibre of your being, the essence of who you are, cries out to do whatever God wants. I mean, everything is all about Him! He is amazing! He is our all in all! However, we will see that Jesus wanted people to be very specific when they asked Him for something. We will look at many scriptures that talk about asking and how to ask. Jesus asked in prayer! We will discuss the Lord's prayer that He taught His disciples after they asked Him to teach them to pray. Then we'll pull it all together and become an asker of the Lord.

We are told many, many times in the New Testament to ask, and we are good at asking the Lord for things in our prayers. When we bring our prayer requests to God, our prayers very often begin with, "Lord, we ask you for...", and this is a very good thing. Jesus tells us in the Gospels to ask.

> "So I say to you, ask, and it will be given to you; seek, and you will find; knock, and it will be opened to you. For everyone who asks, receives, and he who seeks finds, and to him who knocks it will be opened." Luke 11:9-10 (NKJV)

It's very interesting that we can use the word ask as an acronym to remember these words of Jesus from the Gospels. The acronym ASK is Ask, Seek, Knock. In the beginning, God *said.* We are created in His image and His likeness. We are to use our words. We are to ask.

> "Ask and you shall receive. Seek and you shall find. Knock and it shall be opened to you." Matthew 7:7 (NKJV)

God wants us to come to Him and ask, even though He already knows what's on our minds and what's in our hearts. He desires our fellowship! When we pray, when we ask, we are communicating our desires with the Almighty Trinity and by doing so, by fellowshipping with Him, we are fulfilling *His* desire.

Jesus Asked

The disciples asked Jesus to teach them how to pray because they saw fruit from His prayers. We are going to look at Jesus' High Priestly Prayer because in it He prays for us! He actually talks to the Father about giving us something specific. Before we look at Jesus' request, let's look at several of the verses in the prayer. I highly recommend that you read the whole prayer several times and become familiar with it.

89

> "And now, O Father, glorify Me together with Yourself, with the glory which I had with You before the world was. I have manifested Your name to the men whom You have given Me out of the world. ... I pray for them. ... Holy Father, keep through Your name those whom You have given Me, that they may be one as We are. ... I do not pray for these alone, but also for those who will believe in Me through their word; ... and the glory which You gave Me I have given them, that they may be one just as We are one." John 17: 5-6, 9, 11, 20, 22 (NKJV)

In the first part of His prayer, through verse 19, Jesus was praying for the strength and safety of His disciples because He was going back to the Father. Then, in verse 20, Jesus prays for us! He said, "for all those who will one day believe in Me through their message." We believe in Jesus because of the testimonies that His disciples left for us! And we come to the verse that Jesus specifically referenced His glory to the Father.

> "and the glory which You gave Me I have given them." John 17:22 (NKJV)

I had read this scripture many times over many decades before it jumped out at me. Jesus gave us the glory that He shared with the Father! When I realized that I thought, "Nah! Not God's glory. He doesn't share that with anyone! Must be a different word." So I searched the word. It's the same Greek root word used in verse five, and the very same word that Jesus used to describe His glory in verse twenty-four. It's also the same root of the word used for us in the second chapter of Hebrews. Doxa.

"And now, O Father, glorify Me together
with Yourself, with the **glory** which I had
with You before the world was. ... And the
glory which You gave Me I have given them,
... that they may behold My **glory** which
You have given Me." John 17: 5, 22, 24 (NKJV) emphasis mine

"In bringing many sons and daughters to
glory, it was fitting that God, for whom and
through whom everything exists, should make
the pioneer of their salvation perfect through
what he suffered." Hebrews 2:10 (NIV) emphasis mine

Let's look at the verse about God and His glory that's
probably most familiar to us. We
find it in the book of Isaiah where
God says that He will share His
glory with no one. This is why the
verse in John is a bit confusing. If
God said He would share His
glory with no one, then why did
Jesus give it to us? If we read
this verse from Isaiah in it's
entirety, we realize that God is
talking about idols. He doesn't
share His glory with idols. Israel
was not to bow down to idols in

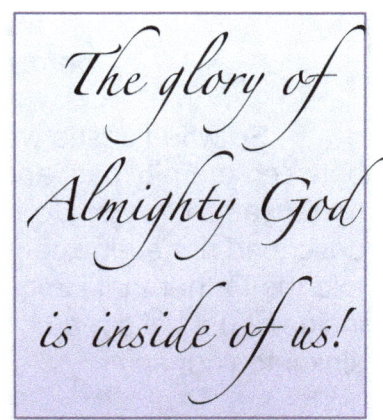

The glory of Almighty God is inside of us!

their homes and then come and bring their sacrifices to the
temple.

"I am the LORD, that is My name; and
My glory I will not give to another, nor
My praise to carved images." Isaiah 42: 8 (NKJV)

There is an odd scripture in the Psalms that correlates
with glory and the worship of idols. In this verse, the Psalmist
is saying that when men bow down and worship idols
(carved images), they give their glory away. This indicates

91

that humans have glory. Think about it. If humans are created in God's image and God has glory, doesn't it stand to reason that humans were created with glory?

> "They made a calf in Horeb, and worshipped the molded image, thus they changed their glory into the image of an ox that eats grass."
> Psalm 106: 19-20 (NKJV)

When Jesus reconciled all creation to Himself by His finished work on the cross and His resurrection, He gave humans back their glory. But much more than that!

He gave to us the glory that He had with the Father before the world was!

So when Jesus was standing on that precipice between eternity past and His declaration of "Light be!", there was a glory of God Almighty that really cannot be described nor even known. But this is the glory that Jesus told the Father that He gave to us. The glory of God dwells inside of us! Let's read it again and let these words of Jesus sink into your spirit.

> "And the glory which You gave Me I have given them, that they may be one just as We are one: I in them, and You in Me; that they may be made perfect in one, and that the world may know that You have sent Me, and have loved them as You have loved Me."
> John17: 22-23 (NKJV)

The Disciples Asked

Jesus' disciples asked Him to teach them how to pray. They saw His devotion to prayer. They knew He got up very early to get alone to pray. They saw that He got answers to His prayers. They saw the miracles He performed and they tied His abilities to His prayer life. They hungered to be more like Him and they knew that prayer was one of the keys. Jesus taught His disciples to pray a very specific prayer.

> "Our Father in heaven, hallowed be Your name. Your kingdom come. Your will be done on earth as it is in heaven. Give us this day our daily bread. And forgive us our debts, as we forgive our debtors. And do not lead us into temptation, but deliver us from the evil one. For Yours is the kingdom and the power and the glory forever. Amen."
> Matthew 6:9-13 (NKJV)

If you will notice both kingdom and heaven are mentioned twice in this short prayer. Your kingdom come. Who's kingdom is He talking about? Father God's kingdom. Another way of saying that is the kingdom of God. The second kingdom phrase can be explained in a similar way. For Yours is the kingdom. Turn this phrase around and you have, the kingdom is Yours. Yours is referring to Our Father, Almighty God. So then we have the second way of saying the kingdom of God.

It's interesting that Jesus will sometimes speak on the kingdom of God and sometimes on the kingdom of heaven. They seem to be

Prayer is a key that opens the kingdom of God.

93

interchangeable. And heaven is the other word that is used twice in this short, powerful prayer. Our Father is in heaven, that is the eternal realm in which He dwells. And then Jesus asks the Father that His kingdom and His will would be on earth as it is in heaven.

Now what do you think heaven is like? Perfection? Peaceful? Joyful? Pain free? Stress free? Overflowing with anything you could desire? And Jesus is teaching His disciples to ask Father God to bring His kingdom realm to earth just the same as it is in heaven.

Think about it. In this eternal, present moment, we are seated with Jesus in the heavenly realm. In our physical reality, we can be sitting on our couch, in our cars, walking in the park, or whatever we want to do, but in the spirit realm we are seated with Jesus. We are in that overlay of the worldly realm and the kingdom of God simultaneously.

We are the connection that Jesus prayed for!
"Your kingdom come, Your will be done
on earth as it is in heaven."

Blind Bartimaeus Asked

"…As He went out of Jericho with His disciples and a great multitude, blind Bartimaeus, the son of Timaeus, sat by the road begging. And when he heard that it was Jesus of Nazareth, he began to cry out and say, 'Jesus, Son of David, have mercy on me!' Then many warned him to be quiet; but he cried out all the more, 'Son of David, have mercy on me!' So Jesus stood still and commanded him to be called. Then

94

they called the blind man, saying to him, 'Be
of good cheer. Rise. He is calling you.' And
throwing aside his garment, he rose and came
to Jesus. So Jesus answered and said to him,
'What do you want Me to do for you?' The blind
man said to Him, "Rabboni, that I may receive
my sight.' Then Jesus said to him, 'Go your way;
your faith has made you well.' And immediately
he received his sight and followed Jesus on
the road." Mark 10: 46-52 (NKJV)

Now when blind Bartimaeus came to Jesus, don't you think it's kind of obvious what the **blind** man wanted? In other scriptures, Jesus knew what the scribes and pharisees were thinking and He knew what the disciples were talking about. Did He not know what this blind man wanted?

> "So Jesus answered and said to him,
> 'What do you want Me to do for you?'"
> Mark 10:51a (NKJV)

Might Jesus have been digging a bit deeper in order to get the blind man to partner with Him in the miracle? Maybe Jesus just wanted Bartimaeus to articulate what he desired? Whatever His reason, Jesus wanted him to **ask.**

> "The blind man said to Him, 'Rabboni, that
> I may receive my sight.'" Mark 10:51b (NKJV)

At the beginning of this story, the people around Bartimaeus tried to get him to be quiet. They shushed him. But he cried out even louder. He was not going to let the Messiah pass him by! The term Son of David is an idiom for the Messiah. And at the end of this story, Bartimaeus followed Jesus on the road. He became one of Jesus' followers, one of His disciples. It is very possible that Bartimaeus was with Jesus at the triumphal entry into Jerusalem and also with the disciples in the upper chamber when the Holy Spirit was given! Batimaeus did not allow the crowd to hush him up. No! Actually he cried out all the louder. Do you sometimes feel that society is trying to shush you? Don't let yourself be shushed! More importantly, don't shush yourself! James, the half-brother of Jesus, also tells us to ask.

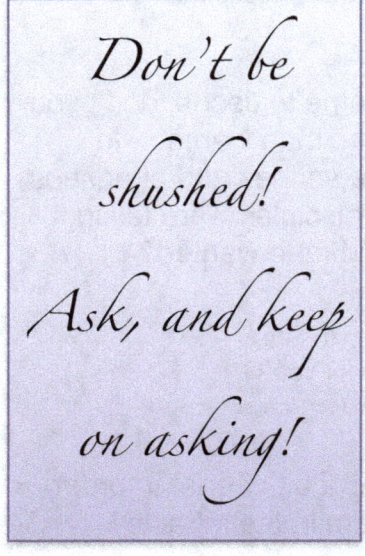

Don't be shushed! Ask, and keep on asking!

"You do not have because you do not ask." James 4:2b (NKJV)

Have you ever been in a situation where you either needed help or wanted company, but you just plugged along alone? Later, while you were talking with a friend and you mentioned the need you had had, did they say, "Oh! I wish you had called me! I was sitting home wanting something to do!" This has happened to me on numerous occasions. One thing I have realized, people want to be asked for help or to go somewhere. Many times we are hoping someone will ask us to go out to lunch and they may be sitting home hoping someone will call and ask them!

Be an Asker!

ASK! Are you an asker? Here is an analogy of GrandMa's cookie jar. There are 3 groups of people when it comes to GrandMa's cookie jar.

1) There are the ones who will go get cookies anytime they want. They risk getting caught and getting in trouble, but that's okay by them.

2) There are the ones who ask GrandMa if they can have a cookie. They risk being told no, but the cookies they do get are freely given to them with no bad conscience.

3) Then there are the kids like I was. We wait patiently in the corner until GrandMa asks us if we would like to have a cookie. We risk getting fewer cookies, but we rarely get into trouble.

My mother was the baby of ten children. When she was around five years old, she was the flower girl in her oldest sister's wedding. By the time I came along my grandmother already had seventeen grandchildren and several great-grandchildren. Any time we would visit, there would be several aunts, uncles, and cousins at Little Mama's house to see their Pollye and her family.

On one such visit, I must have been the only other person in the house besides Little Mama. We were in the kitchen and she asked me if I wanted some ice cream. I was about eight or nine years old and I said, "Yes, ma'am." I remember her putting the ice cream in front of me on the table and she sat down opposite me. The ice cream was butter pecan. I would never have tried it if it hadn't been such a special occasion on such an ordinary day. I liked it. Little Mama told me it was her favorite kind of ice cream and then and there it became my favorite also. I always think of my Little Mama when I eat ice cream and I always order our favorite—butter pecan.

But usually GrandMa is too busy with the other kids to notice us quiet ones. And let's be realistic. GrandMa cannot read minds. She has NO IDEA that the child who doesn't ask for a cookie even wants one! If you are one of the quiet children like I was, step out of your comfort zone and become an asker! The difference between God and GrandMa is that God knows what we need before we ask! But He still wants us to ask!

"For your Father knows the things you have need of before you ask Him." Matt 6:8b (NKJV)

We looked at Matthew 7: 7 and Luke 11: 9-10 earlier in this chapter. They both say that whoever asks, receives, and whoever seeks finds, and whoever knocks, to that person it will be opened! The royal, godly treasure hunt is free and open to all! ASK and keep on asking! Jesus told us to ask many times in the Gospels. Here are a few more verses where Jesus told His followers to ask.

"And whatever you ask in My name, that I will do, that the Father may be glorified in the Son." John 14:13 (NKJV)

"If you ask anything in My name, I will do it." John 14:14 (NKJV)

"If you abide in Me, and My words abide in you, you will ask what you desire, and it shall be done for you." John 15:7 (NKJV)

"...that whatever you ask the Father in My name He may give you." John 15:16b (NKJV)

"And whatever things you ask in prayer, believing, you will receive." Matthew 21:22 (NKJV)

"Most assuredly, I say to you, whatever you ask the Father in My name He will give you. ... Ask, and you will receive, that your joy may be full." John 16:23-24 (NKJV)

Asking with Agreement Prayer

Matthew is the only gospel that records "agreement" prayer. Agreement prayer is basically when you ask someone to pray with you. Usually it's about a specific prayer request.

> "If two of you agree on earth concerning anything they ask, it will be done for them by My Father in heaven." Matthew 18:19 (NKJV)

With what we are learning about prayer, it's important that the person you ask to agree with you in prayer actually DOES agree with you for the intended outcome. You don't want an agreement person who always ends with, "but God if this is not Your will, then may Your will be done." Of course we want God's will for our lives and prayer outcomes, but this ending to a prayer is usually indicative of someone who doesn't really believe in what they are praying for. It's the wishy-washy ending that James mentions in his letter. We will delve into God's will in depth in the next chapter, but right now, don't jeopardize your prayer with a negative prayer partner. Hold you prayers like a beautiful treasure that you only want to show to very special people.

Your prayers are a beautiful treasure. Share them only with special people.

99

Here are two more scriptures that talk about two working together and getting better outcomes because of multiplicity. When you ask someone for prayer, you have also given them the right to ask you about that prayer. This would include any follow through needed on your part. They would be considered an accountability partner with you in this prayer.

"Though one may be overpowered by another, two can withstand him. And a threefold cord is not quickly broken."
Ecclesiastes 4:12 (NKJV)

"How could one chase a thousand, and two put ten thousand to flight, unless their Rock has sold them, and the Lord had surrendered them?" Deuteronomy 32:30 (NKJV)

I am a very strong introvert. I enjoy being alone and doing things by myself. I have commented many times about how many months I could stay home and never leave. Honestly, the Covid lockdown was very easy for me! I had the weight of "I should probably go somewhere" taken off my shoulders! I know that's very weird, but I am a homebody and it was refreshing to stay home with no guilt for the first three months or so!

At the same time, I know that in God's Kingdom, we are the body of Christ. We are not meant to live life alone, but rather we are to live in community. This is why it is so important to have a group of like minded believers that you get together with on a regular basis. We need one another. When we share life with others, we can pray for one another and we can help bear one another's burdens. Sometimes it helps just talking about things and knowing that someone is praying with and for you.

Practicing His Presence

1) Take out your prayer list. Ask God for every request on it. Then just sit with Him and seek Him about those prayer requests. Listen to your heart. Write down any ideas that may come to you. Now make a fist and knock on something as though you were knocking on the door. Hold your prayer list up and say, "Jesus? I'm asking! I'm seeking! I'm knocking!" Have fun with this!

2) Read Jesus' High Priestly Prayer in John 17.

3) On earth as it is in heaven. Think about this phrase from the Lord's Prayer. Is there any aspect of your life where you get a glimpse of heaven? For me, brilliant colors in nature, a sunrise or sunset, rainbows, the scent of flowers in the air, sometimes the way a shaft of light falls across an object, a smile from a stranger, and the eyes of my grandchildren lighting up when they see me give me a feeling of the pure joy of heaven.

4) Pick apart the Lord's Prayer and examine the different phrases. Do other scriptures come to mind as you read it?

5) Are there any items on your prayer list that you would like to have someone agree with you concerning it?

Notes

Chapter 7
Is it God's Will?

There have been times in each of our lives when we've prayed for God's will to be done. Or maybe there were times when we've felt like we were right in the middle of God's will. Or perhaps we've felt like we were as far away from God's will as we could possibly get. We are going to look at some things that the Bible tells us are definitely God's will for each and every one of us. Wouldn't it be great to know that at least in one part of our lives we are walking in His will?

Did you know that He wants us to sit with Him in heavenly places? We'll also explore the idea of waiting on the Lord. Is it God's will to heal? Is it His will to heal us? We shall discuss how something that would bring God pleasure would perhaps be God's will in our lives. We will learn how to know God's will, discern if a thing might be God's will, and ultimately not walk in worry about whether or not we are in God's will.

> *Be empowered to discern God's will as you live a beautiful life.*
>
> Romans 12:2

Obviously, there is a lot of confusion around is it God's will. A lot of times we are waiting on the Lord for His perfect will. What exactly does that mean? It sounds pious and holy, but what does it mean? Is it just a procrastination tactic? I have personal experience in the procrastination arena! "I'm

103

just waiting on God's perfect will." If God created humans in His image, and then died and rose again so that His image-bearers could gain access to His throne room, doesn't it make sense that part of His will is to have a relationship with those He loves and calls His own? Paul tells us this very thing in his letter to the Romans. Let's look at it in two translations.

"And do not be conformed to this world,
but be transformed by the renewing of your
mind, that you may prove what is that good
and acceptable and perfect will of God."
Romans 12:2 (NKJV)

"Stop imitating the ideals and opinions of
the culture around you, but be inwardly
transformed by the Holy Spirit through a
total reformation of how you think. This will
empower you to discern God's will as you
live a beautiful life, satisfying and perfect in
his eyes." Romans 12:2 (TPT)

"As you live a beautiful life." Isn't this a marvelous phrase? I want to live a beautiful life, don't you? I believe that Paul is saying that living such a life is God's will for us, but that this way of life comes with renewing our thinking. Let's see how we can move ourselves and our thoughts toward a beautiful life in Christ Jesus.

Seated with Jesus

If we sit with the Lord in the heavenly realm and we have the mind of Christ, we should be able to answer the question 'is it God's will?' fairly easily. I know we've discussed this idea of being seated with Jesus, the Christ, in heavenly places in earlier chapters, but let's delve into this on a deeper level. The book of Hebrews gives us a glimpse into this heavenly realm where Jesus is seated with Almighty God on the throne.

> "Now this is the main point of the things
> we are saying: We have such a High Priest,
> who is seated at the right hand of the throne
> of the Majesty in the heavens, a Minister
> of the sanctuary and of the true tabernacle
> which the Lord erected, and not man."
> Hebrews 8:1-2 (NKJV)

> "But this Man, after He had offered one
> sacrifice for sins forever, sat down at the
> right hand of God, from that time waiting
> till His enemies are made His footstool. For
> by one offering He has perfected forever
> those who are being sanctified." Hebrews 10:12-14 (NKJV)

Jesus is this Man Who went into the tabernacle in heaven and carried His blood into the heavenly Holy of Holies to offer His sacrifice for sins once and for all! Amen! He is our High Priest. He not only created the universe, but He also created the plan to reconcile all things to Himself with the sacrifice of His life. He created the plan. Remember, He knows the ending from the beginning. Before He said, "Light be!," He was the Lamb Who was slain from the foundation of the world.

This was His plan.
He wanted us to be with Him.

In his letter to the Ephesians, Paul says this very clearly.

> "He chose us to be His very own, joining
> us to Himself even before He laid the
> foundation of the universe!" Ephesians 1:4 (TPT)

The book of the Revelation is a strange writing to say the least. Apocalyptic visions and dreams are full of allegory and metaphor, but they are also mixed with literal reality. If the heavenly realm is outside of our timeframe, one has to ask if this Revelation of Jesus is linear or have parts of it already happened? It is a fascinating book to read, and it is the only book of the Bible that says that those who read it are blessed!

I love the first few chapters. The description of Jesus standing in the middle of the seven golden lampstands is awe inspiring! Let's read this particular account of Jesus now.

Blessed is he who reads and those who hear the words of this prophecy

Rev 1: 3a (NKJV)

"Then I turned to see the voice that spoke with me. And having turned I saw seven golden lampstands, and in the midst of the seven lampstands *One* like the Son of Man, clothed with a garment down to the feet and girded about the chest with a golden band. His head and hair *were* white like wool, as white as snow, and His eyes like a flame of fire; His feet *were* like fine brass, as if refined in a furnace, and His voice as the sound of many waters; He had in His right hand seven stars, out of His mouth went a sharp two-edged sword, and His countenance was like the sun shining in its strength." Revelation 1: 12-16 (NKJV)

A similar description is found in the book of Daniel. We can see from these verses that to try to put words to the indescribable God falls short of His glory and magnificence. But, oh! what wonderfully difficult descriptions these are!

"I watched till thrones were put in place, and the Ancient of Days was seated; His garment *was* white as snow, and the hair of His head *was* like pure wool. His throne *was* a fiery flame, its wheels a burning fire; a fiery stream issued and came forth from before Him. A thousand thousands ministered to Him; ten thousand times ten thousand stood before Him. The court was seated, and the books were opened. ... I was watching in the night visions, and behold, *One* like the Son of Man, coming with the clouds of heaven! He came to the Ancient of Days, and they brought Him near before Him. Then to Him was given dominion and glory and a kingdom, that all peoples, nations, and languages should serve Him. His dominion *is* an everlasting dominion, which shall not pass away, and His kingdom *the one* which shall not be destroyed."

Daniel 7: 9-10; 13-14 (NKJV)

The following verse in the third chapter of the book of Revelation is used a lot for altar calls. However, this part of the chapter was written to the church in Thyatira. It was written to people who were already followers of Jesus. Pay attention to this invitation from our Lord. Not only does He want to come into our lives and eat with us (which can be a metaphor for a deep, meaningful relationship or friendship), He also wants us to sit with Him on His throne. You are an overcomer, my friend!

"Behold, I stand at the door and knock. If anyone hears My voice and opens the door, I will come in to him and dine with him, and he with Me. To him who overcomes

107

I will grant to sit with Me on My throne, as I
also overcame and sat down with My Father
on His throne." Rev 3: 20-21 (NKJV)

Remember when we discussed the Lord's Prayer?
Think about the part that says,"Thy kingdom come Thy will
be done on earth as it is in heaven." Jesus is the One Who
opened heaven to His image-bearers. Why did He do that?
According to this prayer that He taught His disciples, it was
so that God's will would be done on earth as it is in heaven!

We are His image-bearers on earth!
We are the connection of
on earth as it is in heaven!

We are living in the physical realm of the created
earth, clothed in these human jars of clay—our bodies. At
the same time, the Spirit of the living God dwells inside us.

This makes us an integral part of the invisible
overlay of the Kingdom of God.
In His Spirit, we live *on earth as it is in heaven*!

Now, I know that this next verse out of Revelation is
more specific to John and his vision, but let's think about it in
terms of us being invited by Jesus to sit with Him in heavenly
places. Then we shall pair this verse to the one from
Ephesians that follows it. The Ephesians verse explicitly
says that God raised us up and made us sit in heavenly
places in Christ Jesus.

"After these things I looked, and behold, a
door standing open in heaven. And the first
voice which I heard was like a trumpet
speaking with me, saying, 'Come up here,
and I will show you things which must take
place after this.'" Rev 4:1 (NKJV)

108

"But God, who is rich in mercy, because of His great love with which He loved us, even when we were dead in trespasses, made us alive together with Christ (by grace you have been saved), and raised us up together, and made us sit together in the heavenly places in Christ Jesus, that in the ages to come He might show the exceeding riches of His grace in His kindness toward us in Christ Jesus."

Ephesians 2: 4-7 (NKJV)

Connecting all these Scriptures together gives us a picture of God's plan of salvation. He knew His plan before He ever created humans in His image. He wants you seated with Him.

"You will show me the path of life; in Your presence is fullness of joy; at Your right hand are pleasures forevermore."

Psalm 16: 11 (NKJV)

"looking unto Jesus, the author and finisher of our faith, who for the joy that was set before Him endured the cross, despising the shame, and has sat down at the right hand of the throne of God." Hebrews 12: 2 (NKJV)

So think about it. Where is Jesus seated? He's seated at the right hand of God. Where did God raise us up to? He made us sit together in the heavenly places in Christ Jesus. Where is Jesus? At the right hand of God. Where are we seated in the heavenly realm? In Jesus. What caused Jesus to endure the cross? The joy that

Salvation

The Divine Mystery

109

was set before Him. What was that joy? US! He wanted to reconcile us to God! What's at God's right hand? Pleasures forevermore. And? Jesus! And? We are seated with Jesus!

We are the joy of Jesus and God's pleasures at His right hand forevermore! It's not up to us to decide if we're worthy or not to sit with Jesus in heavenly places.

It's God's plan.
Take your place beside Him.
Ask Him what His will is.

Then listen.

The Will of God

There is a verse in Thessalonians that tells us directly what God's will is for our lives. Say what? Really? We looked at it earlier, but let's dig deeper into this Scripture.

> "Rejoice always, pray without ceasing, in everything give thanks; for this is the will of God in Christ Jesus concerning you." 1 Thessalonians 5:16 (NKJV)

This verse is not saying that everything that happens is God's will, but rather that we should be thankful people, rejoicing people, and praying people, no matter what happens. We are going to deconstruct this verse a bit to find the will of God for our lives. The last part of this verse says "for this is the will of God in Christ Jesus concerning you."

Concerning who? YOU! The will of God! In Christ Jesus! Concerning YOU! So what is the will of God for us according to the rest of this verse?

Rejoice Always

Rejoice always. Does that mean only when I'm happy? Rejoicing is easy to do when things are going well, but this verse says to ALWAYS REJOICE. There is a place in Jesus where the "joy of the Lord" truly is our strength.

This verse from Nehemiah is really an interesting look into the joy of the Lord. It had been 70 years since Jerusalem and the Temple had been destroyed. Many Israelites had been living in Babylon all that time. Many others were scattered among other nations. There were no sacrifices, because there was no Temple. Daniel had prophesied that at the end of 70 years, the people would return. Ezra and Nehemiah had realized that those 70 years of Babylonian captivity were up and they went back to Jerusalem. Ezra to rebuild a Temple and Nehemiah to rebuild the wall surrounding the city.

Let the joy of the Lord lead you into His peace that passes understanding.

They had gathered the people together at the beginning of the building process to read the Book of the Law. For many of them, this may have been the first time they heard the law. Evidently the words cut them to their core. Nehemiah 8, verse 9 says, "For all the people wept, when they heard the words of the Law." Then Nehemiah gave them the next directive from which the "joy of the Lord" comes.

> "Then he said to them, 'Go your way, eat the fat, drink the sweet, and send portions to those for whom nothing is prepared; for this day is holy to our Lord. Do not sorrow, for the joy of the Lord is your strength.'" Nehemiah 8:10 (NKJV)

This is not a surface happiness or a joy of the moment, but a very deep, inner joy of being one with our Savior and God. In the Gospel of John, Jesus told us what to do when we go through trying times.

> "These things I have spoken to you, that in Me you may have peace. In the world you will have tribulation; but BE OF GOOD CHEER, I have overcome this world." John 16:33 (NKJV) (emphasis mine)

Do you know anyone in this world who has not experienced tribulation? Everyone has and everyone does, but Jesus said to be cheerful no matter what! Another way of saying be of good cheer would be to say rejoice always! Remember this is the will of God—to always rejoice!

> "Rejoice in the Lord always. Again I will say, rejoice! Let your gentleness be known to all men. The Lord is at hand. Be anxious for nothing, but in everything by prayer and supplication, with thanksgiving, let your requests be made known to God; and the

peace of God, which surpasses all understanding, will guard your hearts and minds through Christ Jesus." Phil 4:4-7 (NKJV)

So, according to these scriptures, if you're not rejoicing, you're not walking in God's will. This is extremely simplistic and very black and white. My daughter always pushes back at me when I say this because there are some people whose brain wiring makes them more anxious about things. Honestly, I think I am one of these people, but brain wiring is not what I'm talking about here. I am using a broad brush stroke and hopefully you will begin to consciously rejoice even when you don't feel like it. If you find yourself anxious about being anxious and trying not to be anxious, don't worry about it. Chill out. There are gray areas in this learning to rejoice process.

Be of good cheer! Jesus has overcome this world!

I totaled my car a few years ago. I hydroplaned on a bridge. It was a single car accident. I was NOT rejoicing about losing that car! I really liked that car! And I didn't even get trade-in value for it! I was NOT rejoicing about that AT ALL. However, I did rejoice that I walked away without a scratch and never had any soreness! The car was so damaged that the appraiser stopped counting how much it would take to repair. The only place that was not damaged was my driver's seat. The car wreck was not God's will. It happened. Things happen. My choice to find something in that wreck to rejoice about was God's will.

Pray Without Ceasing

To pray without ceasing means to never stop praying. Oh my! Does this verse really mean that we are to constantly pray? What about when we eat? We're not supposed to talk with our mouths full! I pray in my car when I am alone, sometimes for a couple of hours at a time, but then I may just want to listen to some music. Does that mean that I have ceased praying? What about sleeping? Should I stay awake all night every night so that I can constantly pray? Do you see how silly it can get when we look at some verses literally?

If you remember, prayer is communication with God. We communicate in many different ways, sometimes only with our eyes or gestures. To pray without ceasing is more

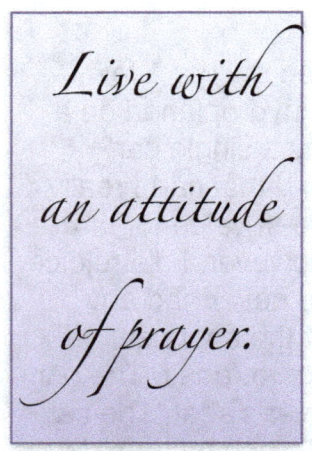

Live with

an attitude

of prayer.

like being aware that our Lord is with us at all times. When I am in my house with my spouse or one of my children, I don't sit with them all the time and just talk to them. I would never get anything done and they would get very tired of me! However, the Creator of the Universe, the One Who holds all things together, can sit with each and every one of us all the time! As we realize His presence with us, as we begin to think about Him walking beside us everywhere we go, we are stepping into that silent communication of being with someone you trust and love.

In Everything Give Thanks

In everything give thanks for this is the will of God. This does not say that we give thanks *for* everything. It says to give thanks *in* everything.

Circumstances happen to each and every one of us that we wish had not occurred. When my car accident happened, my car came to a stop on the shoulder of the interstate facing the oncoming traffic. I had hydroplaned on a bridge, and as my vehicle was spinning and I had zero control, I looked up and said, "Jesus?" I knew if another vehicle hit me at interstate speeds, I was going to see my Maker. After the car stopped, I was looking at the cars going by and all I could say was, "Thank You!" I was thankful that I was alive. I was thankful that I didn't hit anyone. I was thankful that no one hit me. I was thankful that I wasn't hurting. I was NOT thankful that my car looked pretty much totaled to me. So, I was not thankful *for* the circumstance, but I was very thankful *in* the circumstance. Does that make sense?

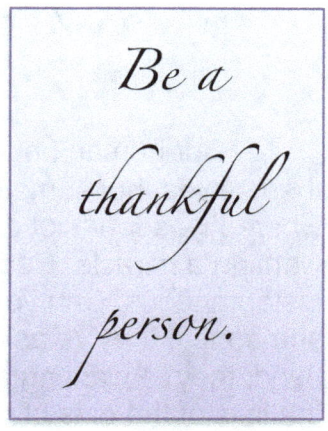

Be a thankful person.

"Rejoice always, pray without ceasing, in everything give thanks; for this is the will of God in Christ Jesus concerning you." 1 Thessalonians 5:16 (NKJV)

This Thessalonians verse is really talking about our lifestyle of moving with God through our daily lives. We learn to rejoice throughout our days. We learn to walk in communication with Jesus all throughout each and every day. We learn to be truly thankful and grateful people for the smallest of things in our lives. This is the will of God in Christ Jesus concerning you.

What about Healing?

Our human bodies are designed to heal by themselves, but sometimes they need help. This is an area where I've seen a lot of people pray for healing, but they're wanting a miracle. Healing happens over time. Miracles are instantaneous. Can you see how confusing it would be to someone if they've asked for prayer for healing, but in their mind, they're wanting an instantaneous miracle? In one of the lists of the gifts of the Spirit healing and miracles are listed separately.

> "But the manifestation of the Spirit is given to each one for the profit of all: ...to another gifts of healing by the same Spirit, to another the working of miracles,..."
>
> 1 Corinthians 12:7-9 (NKJV) (emphasis mine)

In my life, I've seen a lot of healing, I've seen a lot of miracles, and I've seen some miracles of healing. I've been privileged to pray for a lot of people and I've watched a lot of people get prayed for. I've seen people who are praying for healing, but they don't believe it will happen, they are just hoping that it might. I've seen people who pray for healing, and as an act of faith, they throw away their medicine or glasses and then find themselves in an emergency situation.

Then they blame God that it didn't happen or they say that He wanted them to learn a lesson.

God did not create sickness and disease in anyone's body to teach them something. Sometimes people learn from a time of ailment and healing, but usually it's because they have had to cease all their busy work. They have time to read the Bible, pray, and press into their relationship with Jesus. That is a great thing, but God did not give them sickness so that they would get closer to Him. Jesus tells us where all the bad stuff we encounter comes from.

> "The thief does not come except to steal, and to kill, and to destroy. I have come that they may have life, and that they may have it more abundantly." John 10:10 (NKJV)

> "A thief has only on thing in mind—he wants to steal, slaughter, and destroy. But I have come to give you everything in abundance, more than you expect—life in its fullness until you overflow!" John 10:10 (TPT)

We live in a society where we can easily go to a doctor for treatment of any ailment. I have come to see our American medical treatment as a miraculous establishment. Many people are living healthy lives who would not have survived a few short decades ago. God does heal supernaturally, but He also uses our modern, miraculous medical establishment and alternative care. When you pray for healing, ask God for wisdom also. Your healing may come through your doctor!

In 1999, I awakened feeling a little sick to my stomach. And then happened. It was almost as though I heard the explosion with my ears. My appendix had ruptured. I remember lying there waiting for the pain to subside so I could wake up my husband. He got up before I said anything and headed toward his closet. "Where are you going?" I wailed. "I'm taking you to the emergency room!" I thought I was being quiet, but evidently not! I am very grateful for the morphine that took the pain away, but I'm more grateful for the surgery that probably saved my life!

Jesus made an interesting statement in Luke and I believe we can assume this is always His will toward healing. A leper had come up to Him to ask Him for healing. Lepers were outcasts of society and were not supposed to approach anyone for anything. It was a highly contagious disease with no effective treatment. No one wanted to be around them and no one wanted to touch them. They could not go to a physician for help because there was no help for leprosy at that time like there is now.

> "And it happened when He was in a certain city, that behold, a man who was full of leprosy saw Jesus; and he fell on his face and implored Him, saying, 'Lord, if You are willing, You can make me clean.' Then He put out His hand and touched him, saying, "I am willing; be cleansed. Immediately the leprosy left him." Luke 5: 12-13 (NKJV)

God was willing not only to heal this outcast of society, but also to reach out and touch him! Again, sickness and disease are part of the curse. They are not God's will for humans. When God created, He looked at His creation and said, "It is good." Then the great rebellion occurred and the curse hit His wonderful creation.

Because Jesus knew the ending before He created the beginning, He knew the curse would happen. That's why His plan was to die on the cross and rise victoriously from the grave so that by His actions He would reconcile, not only His image-bearers to Himself, but all of creation.

> "...and healed all who were sick, that it might be fulfilled which was spoken by

Isaiah the prophet, saying: 'He Himself
took our infirmities and bore our sicknesses.'"
Matthew 8: 16b-17 (NKJV)

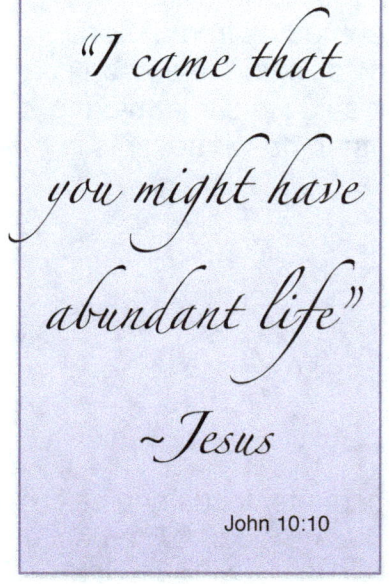

"I came that you might have abundant life"

~Jesus

John 10:10

The ultimate goal in praying for healing is to be healed by any and every means. Understand that infirmities come from the curse, never from God. Always pray for healing, but do what you can to help the healing process of your body. Isaiah gives us a picture of Jesus on the cross, not only dying for sins, but also for healing.

"But He was wounded for our
transgressions, He was bruised
for our iniquities; the chastisement
for our peace was upon Him,
and by His stripes we are healed."
Isaiah 53: 5 (NKJV)

The Apostle Peter quoted Isaiah in his first letter. Think about this. Peter watched Jesus being interrogated in the house of the High Priest. That's where Peter denied knowing Jesus. In the books of Matthew and Mark, we see that Peter was an eyewitness to Jesus being beaten. In the second chapter of Acts, we see the fisherman Peter filled with courage and quoting scripture to the inhabitants of Israel. Can you just imagine as Peter penned these words, quoting from the prophet Isaiah, that he was remembering his witness of this prophecy coming true?

"who Himself bore our sins in His own body
on the tree, that we, having died to sins,
might live for righteousness—by whose
stripes you were healed." 1 Peter 2: 24 (NKJV)

When I pray for healing, I always pray for life. John 10:10 is my go to verse. I pray for things that are trying to steal, kill, or destroy the person or situation to cease and desist because they have no right in a believer's life. They are part of the curse that Jesus redeemed us from. Then I pray for life and life more abundantly to fill up the person or situation because that is what Jesus said He came to bring us! Always pray for life and healing, then do whatever is in your ability to do about the illness.

What about Things?

Think back to the leper who came to Jesus and said, "Lord, if You are willing, You can make me clean." The desire of this man's heart was to be healed. If he were healed, he could go home to his family. He could see his friends. He could enjoy holidays with his community. Jesus' desire was to answer this man's prayer, to give him the desire of his heart, to give him his life back! Isn't that awesome? When we pray about family, friends, jobs, things, you name it, every thing we pray about, there is something in that prayer that is a desire of our heart.

> "Delight yourself also in the Lord, and He
> shall give you the desires of your heart."
> Psalm 37:4 (NKJV)

Earlier we touched on God giving us the desires of our heart if we delight ourselves in Him. We asked Him to show us the desires of our hearts and we started a list of what those desires are. We've seen scripture after scripture where desperate people came to Jesus and their only desire was for healing for themselves or a loved one. Can you see how connected our prayers are whether they're for healing, desires of our hearts, or other things? Jesus came that we might have an abundant life or life to the full—a beautiful life! So the more our prayers come to fruition the more we're able to live our lives to the full and spread His life and good news to those around us!

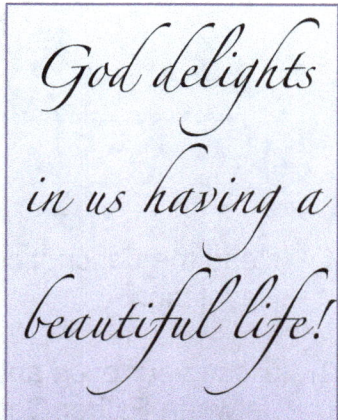

God delights in us having a beautiful life!

Over the past couple of years, Luke 12 has become one of my favorite chapters. There are gems of all kinds in this chapter. One is the fire of God. One is to not worry or have an anxious mind. One is to NOT fear God, because we are worth more than the sparrows that He takes care of! And there's much, much more in this chapter. One verse even talks about how much pleasure it brings to God to give us the kingdom!

> "Do not fear, little flock, for it is your Father's good pleasure to give you the kingdom."
> Luke 12:32 (NKJV)

So IF it brings God PLEASURE to give us the kingdom of God, do you think it gives Him PLEASURE to answer our prayers? We delight in Him and He delights (good pleasure) to give us the kingdom. How much greater is the kingdom of God than anything we could ask for? So why wouldn't God also take good pleasure in answering our prayers? Answered prayer is a desire of my heart!

Practicing His Presence

1) Read the description of Jesus in the first chapter of Revelation.

2) Close your eyes and imagine yourself sitting right between Father God and Jesus. Then see the Holy Spirit hovering over you.

3) Set at least three alarms on your phone. When they go off, rejoice in the Lord for whatever you want to rejoice about.

4) After rejoicing, take a deep breath and just prayerfully contemplate the presence of the Lord.

5) After thinking about Jesus, be thankful. You are in God's will according to 1 Thessalonians 5:16!

6) Look at your prayer list. Is there anything on your list that there would be any reason that your loving, heavenly Father would not want to give you? Read Luke 11:11-13.

Notes

Chapter 8
Cultivate an Abundant Mindset

Our overall outlook on life actually has a lot to do with our faith, belief, and answered prayer. It's the old "do you see the glass half full or half empty" question. Are you an optimist or a pessimist? Are you a positive person or a negative person most of the time? I think you can see a pattern here. What is so incredible is that we can change our overall outlook. We are going to discuss having an abundant mindset as opposed to a poverty mindset. We shall learn how to cultivate an abundant outlook on life! We shall look at several scriptures that speak to this.

When I was a freshman at Vanderbilt, one of my professors actually asked us a question that changed my way of thinking. I don't remember the class, but we were in a huge lecture hall, with at least two hundred students in the class. I was sitting about mid-way up the auditorium. He came on the stage and placed a glass with water in it on the desk. He posed the question. "Is the glass half full or half empty?" Immediately I thought, "It's half empty." He then proceeded to explain to us that people who see the glass half empty have a pessimistic view of life, while the people who see the glass half full have an optimistic view on life. I was seventeen years old and, in a very weird way, this made total sense to me.

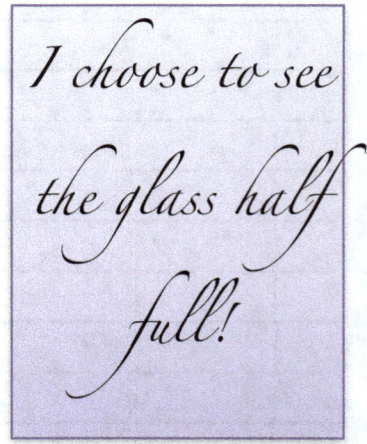

I choose to see the glass half full!

I decided then and there to never again allow myself to see the glass as half empty. It would always be half full! I do have to admit that it took a while to break myself of the habit. I would see a half empty glass. My thoughts would wend their way through his lecture. I would think about it and my feelings of why I saw it half empty instead of half full. Finally I would see the same glass half full. Now I always see them half full! That is an optimist's mindset!

Of course, an abundant mindset cannot be discussed without talking about money. Money is a huge topic and many people have been taught that it is evil, but it isn't! We shall learn how to think about money in its proper perspective. By using a simple scale, you will be able to see what areas of life you are thinking abundantly in and what areas of life need a little help. It's very exciting to me to have a roadmap to become a more optimistic, abundant minded person. I hope you feel the same by the end of this chapter!

Money is a necessity in our society. It's a very good tool to have.

The Robin Hood mentality says we should take from the rich and give to the poor. Basically, thievery! This mentality comes from a finite, poverty mindset that says, "There's not enough to go around." In reality, we live in an amazing, super-abundant world with plenty for everyone. It's poverty mindsets that keep people in poverty. Let's address some of these thoughts and learn how to cultivate an abundant mindset.

We all know negative people. There are some who seem to have the knack of bringing a whole room of happy people to the brink of despair. These are the people who walk around with a gloom and doom atmosphere around them. They would definitely have a poverty mindset. Everything's bad. Nothing is good enough. On the other hand, one would think that the happy, enthusiastic person would naturally have an abundant mindset, but that is not necessarily the case. Have you ever heard a positive person say something to the effect of money doesn't grow on trees? Or the love of money is the root of all evil? To have an abundant mindset, one has to monitor their attitude on a consistent basis.

The One Who has will get More

Jesus said a lot of very odd things. One in particular in Matthew alludes to having a poverty or an abundant mindset. Jesus is explaining the parable of the sower. Let's look at this and a few more scriptures to further understand the importance of our mindsets.

> "For whoever has, to him more will be given, and he will have abundance; but whoever does not have, even what he has will be taken from him." Matthew 13:12 (NKJV)

Really? This sounds a lot like the rich get richer and the poor get poorer. It really sounds extremely unfair. Jesus did not say this in order to explain this particular parable. He said this many times! Let's dig a little deeper into mindsets. Here are a few other examples from His teaching.

> "For to everyone who has, more will be

126

given, and he will have abundance; but from him who does not have, even what he has will be taken away." Matthew 25:29 (NKJV)

"Take heed what you hear. With the same measure you use, it will be measured to you; and to you who hear, more will be given. For whoever has, to him more will be given; but whoever does not have, even what he has will be taken away from him." Mark 4:24-25 (NKJV)

"Therefore take heed how you hear. For whoever has, to him more will be given; and whoever does not have, even what he seems to have will be taken from him."
Luke 8:18 (NKJV)

"For I say to you, that to everyone who has will be given; and from him who does not have, even what he has will be taken away." Luke 19:26 (NKJV)

These Scriptures say that whoever doesn't have even what he has will be taken away from him! That doesn't sound just nor fair! And it isn't if you look at it from worldly, materialistic eyes. Let's look at these scriptures as **mindsets** instead of things.

Imagine someone with a poverty mindset. There is never enough. If something bad can happen, it will. Things always come in three's. When it rains, it

The Eyeores of the world have negative mindsets.

127

pours. "Bad things always happen to me." They seem to have a cloud over them without any silver lining at all. You know you know someone like this. Grumpy to the core.

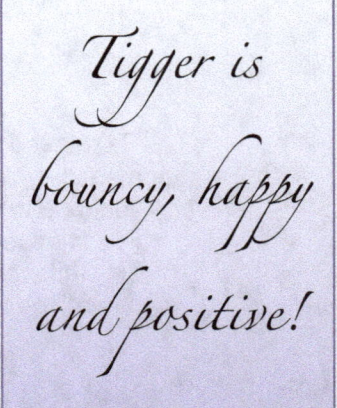

Tigger is bouncy, happy and positive!

Now imagine someone with an abundant mindset. There's plenty to go around. They find the good in every situation. Good things come to those who wait. What a blessing rain is to all the gardens and fields. They light up a room. You want to be around them. They make you feel better. All clouds have silver linings. They just seem blessed. Smiling all the time.

Most of us are Winnie the Pooh, somewhere in the middle.

Let's go back to the Matthew 13 verse and look at it with mindset eyes. For whoever has (an abundant mindset), to him more will be given, and he will have abundance (because he sees abundance everywhere he looks). But whoever does not have (because he has a poverty mindset and there is never enough), even what he has will be taken from him (because it is not enough). I know I'm stretching it a bit here, but bear with me. I want to you think about the people in the above scriptures as having an abundant or a poverty mindset and that is the reason they are given more or what they have is taken away.

Let's look at the Mark verse with the same mindset eyes. Take heed what you hear. What are you listening to? Gloom and doom? Or stories filled with life? With the same measure you use (abundant mindset or poverty mindset), it will be measured to you; and to you who hear, more will be given. More will be given of whichever mindset you listen to! For whoever has (abundant mindset), to him more will be given; but whoever does not have (poverty mindset), even what he has will be taken away from him. Our mindsets affect every part of our lives!

Changing Your Mindset

Several years ago, our children were living in Hawaii, two sons (one married) and two daughters. All were out there for different reasons. The newlyweds decided to start their lives together in a new place. Our soldier son was stationed at Schofield Barracks. Our daughters decided separately that they wanted to move there. One went to have an adventure in living in Hawaii, the other transferred from Palm Beach Atlantic University to Hawaii Pacific University. They each had their own living spaces. My husband and I couldn't join them in Paradise because our parents were aging and we just didn't feel we should leave them. I think our kids were happy we didn't follow them!

Bill and I would vicariously go to Hawaii by watching a very popular TV drama that was set on O'ahu. It was a crime show and most of the story lines were basically violence against women. I was feeding my mind with this garbage and I was all but convinced that our girls were in mortal danger. My peace was disrupted and I was living in fear

129

where my daughters were concerned. I was listening to lies and I finally realized it after a particularly stupid show plot. I haven't watched that show since. In fact, I've been very picky about the shows I watch for entertainment.

There is an old saying, "Birds of a feather flock together." Think about the people you are around most. Are they negative in their words and have a poverty mindset of lack? Or are they positive and have an abundant mindset of more than enough? The people you are with will affect you. And the people you are with the most will affect you the most.

An abundant mindset does not take anything away from someone else.

Unfortunately, it seems like there are many more poverty mindsets in the world than there are abundant mindsets. Our news cycle is definitely a negative mindset. The old news adage "if it bleeds, it leads" is still the rule of thumb for writing headlines in our society.

The good news is we can move into an abundant mindset! The more you work toward having an abundant mindset, the smaller your poverty mindset becomes. These mindsets include material things like money, houses, jobs, cars, etc, but they're not exclusive to only things. They include relationships, health, your outlook on life — you name it and you have a mindset or viewpoint on that particular thing.

Cultivating an Abundant Mindset

Look at this simple scale where a poverty mindset is at zero and an abundant mindset is at 100. This is a fun exercise to see where you are in different areas of your life on this spectrum. Place yourself on this spectrum in the categories of health, relationships, money, career, job, prayer, and other things. When I first learned about the different mindsets, I was between a 35 and 40 on this scale. I had just never thought about it before! I would analyze things and go to the negative side very quickly. Now, many years later, I am between 80 and 90 on this scale. My outlook on life and my enjoyment of life is so much better!

Poverty Mindset		Abundant Mindset
0	50	100

Consider your life with an honest and open mind. Where are you on this spectrum? Wherever you are on this line, decide right now that you are going to be more abundant in your thinking. Right now! Think about the good things in your life and just be grateful they are there. Now think about the goodness of Jesus and be grateful for your relationship with Him. That has moved you more toward an abundant mindset — just by reading this paragraph!

Now think about an area where you know you have a poverty mindset. Something where you feel there's just not enough or you're really dissatisfied and it will never get better. Think about one thing you can do to move that thing in a more positive direction. If you can't think of anything tangible that you can do, then ask Jesus to show you something. Prayer is a very active part of an abundant mindset!

These are the extremes of the mindsets. We are all a mix of both. But, if you could choose one as your predominant mindset, which one would it be? If you think about it, the abundant mindset people are full of peace, joy, and contentment whether their prayers are answered or not. The poverty mindset people are upset and negative even if all their prayers get answered the way they want because **it's never enough.**

So, if we are a mix of both, how do we move toward being more of the abundant mindset and less of the poverty mindset? Think about the scripture in Galatians that talks about the works of the flesh (negative) and the fruit of the Spirit (positive). If we concentrate on becoming more like the fruit of the Spirit, then we don't have as much room in our lives for the works of the flesh.

Love Joy

Peace Patience

Kindness

Goodness

Faithfulness

Gentleness

Self-control

"Now the practices of the sinful nature are clearly evident: they are sexual immorality, impurity, sensuality (total irresponsibility, lack of self-control), idolatry, sorcery, hostility, strife, jealousy, fits of anger, disputes, dissensions, factions [that

promote heresies], envy,
drunkenness, riotous behavior, and other
things like these. I warn you beforehand,
just as I did previously, that those who
practice such things will not inherit the
kingdom of God. But the fruit of the Spirit
[the result of His presence within us] is love
[unselfish concern for others], joy, [inner]
peace, patience [not the ability to wait, but
how we act while waiting], kindness, goodness,
faithfulness, gentleness, self-control."

Galatians 5:19-23 (Amplified)

If we choose to concentrate on the positives of the fruit of the Spirit and adding more of that into our lives, then we don't have as much time or space to think about the negative works of the flesh. Thinking about ways to add the fruit of the Spirit in our lives moves us into a more abundant mindset. What does having an abundant mindset have to do with answered prayer? Think about the Scripture in Mark where Jesus taught about our attitude in prayer.

"When you pray, believe that you've already received, and you'll have whatever you ask for."
Mark 11:24 (NKJV)

All things are possible

~

only believe!

If we are abundant mindset people, we would be more prone to believing that God will answer this for us. We would be more receptive to receiving the answer to our prayer. We would believe and not doubt. However, if we are in a poverty mindset mode in prayer, we would be more prone to disbelieving that God would ever do anything for us! Does that make sense?

133

An abundant mindset sees the abundance of Almighty God, and in that abundance, the answer to their prayers does NOT take away from any one else's prayers. There is infinite supply in God's economy.

When we walk with this understanding, why it is important to have an abundant mindset, we realize that it is not a selfish thing to ask God for more. In fact, abundant mindset people become more generous because they see abundance.

Positive people are more fun to be around!

However, being around people with negative attitudes is not a very pleasant prospect. A poverty mindset person doesn't believe there's enough to go around so they hold on to all their stuff. In case things run out, they'll still have something.

Money

From personal experience with my own prayers and others' prayer requests over the last few decades, prayer for money issues is a huge area. Let's face it, we need money to live in our society. We purchase food, clothing, and shelter with what? MONEY!!! So why does money have such a bad reputation? Part of the answer is a scripture that is usually misquoted as "money is the root of all evil." Let's look at what this verse really says.

> "For the love of money is a root of all kinds of evil, for which some have strayed from the faith in their greediness and pierced themselves through with many sorrows."
>
> 1 Timothy 6:10 (NKJV)

According to this verse, money is not bad, it's the love

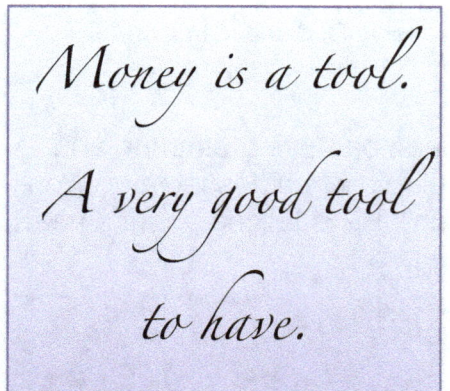

Money is a tool. A very good tool to have.

of money, as in greediness, that's bad. It's not the money itself, it's people's reaction to money. A greedy person would definitely fall into the poverty mindset because they feel there's just not enough to go around and they want more.

There is a Jewish idiom that says someone with a good eye is a generous person and someone with a bad eye is a miserly person. In the Gospel of Matthew, Jesus is teaching on this idiom. A good eye is symbolic of a generous person or a person who has an abundant mindset. A bad eye is symbolic of a miserly person or a person who has a poverty mindset. Therefore if you have a good eye, you are generous with your time, money, and things. You have an abundance mindset. If you have a bad eye, you are miserly and don't share or give anything easily, because there might not be enough left for "me". You have a poverty mindset.

> "The lamp of the body is the eye. If therefore your eye is good, your whole body will be full of light. But if your eye is bad, your whole body will be full of darkness. If therefore the light that

is in you is darkness, how great is that darkness!"
Matthew 6:22-23 (NKJV)

If you have an abundant mindset and you are a generous person, you have a good eye. If you have a poverty mindset and you are a miserly, greedy person, you have a bad eye. This thought process continues with Jesus' subsequent words.

"No one can serve two masters; for either
he will hate the one and love the other, or
else he will be loyal to the one and despise
the other. You cannot serve God and mammon."
Matthew 6:24 (NKJV)

If we use the good eye and bad eye metaphor, and there's no reason why we shouldn't, when Jesus says, "You cannot serve God and mammon", He is talking about a heart issue. We want to serve God with a good eye, very generous and open, but if our view of mammon is with a bad eye, miserly and closed, we cannot be generous in our serving of God. The good eye and bad eye parts of us would always be in conflict. We cannot serve God with a generous mindset and mammon with a miserly mindset at the same time. In the Gospel of Luke, Jesus puts a different spin on the issue of serving God and mammon.

Be generous.

"Therefore if you have not been faithful in
the unrighteous mammon, who will commit
to your trust the true riches? And if you have
not been faithful in what is another man's,
who will give you what is your own? No servant
can serve two masters; for either he will hate
the one and love the other, or else he will be
loyal to the one and despise the other. You
cannot serve God and mammon." Luke 16:11-13 (NKJV)

136

It is interesting that Jesus told His followers that in order to be trusted with the true riches, we must be faithful in the unrighteous mammon. The true riches are the riches we find in Christ and in the kingdom of God. These riches are things that money can't buy. Things like the fruit of the Spirit. Living our lives with a Kingdom of God philosophy. Being seated with Christ in heavenly places. Living life with His peace that surpasses all understanding!

Money is a tool. A tool that we all need in this physical life of ours. Think of money like a hammer in a tool box. If we take care of our tools, if we are faithful in the unrighteous mammon, our tools actually serve us when the time comes. If we take care of our hammer and put it back in

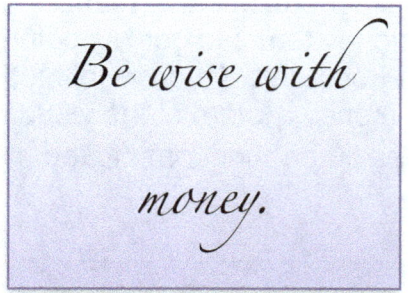

Be wise with money.

it's place in the tool box, we can easily access it to hang a picture. Our hammer serves us when the time comes. With this analogy, if we are faithful with unrighteous mammon, it will serve us when the time comes. We can be trusted with the true riches we find in Christ Jesus.

One of the scriptures used earlier in this chapter was from a parable Jesus told about three men who were entrusted with a wealthy man's business while he went on a journey. Two of the men doubled the finances that were put under their care. The third was scared of the wealthy man and hid the money in order to just give him back what had been given to him to take care of. He didn't even try. The first two men were commended by the wealthy man. Because they had been faithful with what had been given to them, they were given more. The third man was called untrustworthy and lazy. He was told if he had put the money in the bank he would have at least collected interest. His funds were taken away from him and given to the other two men. Then he was banished from the kingdom.

> "For to everyone who has more will be given, and he will have abundance; but from him who does not have, even what he has will be taken away."
> Matthew 25:29 (NKJV)

> "For the one who has will be given more, until he overflows with abundance. And the one with hardly anything, even what little he has will be taken from him."
> Matthew 25:29 (TPT)

Now I know that this parable is ultimately talking about being faithful to the Lord in kingdom, spiritual matters, but He uses very real, concrete money terms to get His point across. This ties in with our verse from Luke. If you're faithful in small matters, the unrighteous money system of the world, you will be faithful in the true riches of the Kingdom of God.

Abundance

In the Gospel of John, Jesus actually said that He came to give us abundant life! Now a lot of people would say this is for our spiritual lives, and I would certainly agree. But it does not exclude our financial lives. As a side note, Jesus is also telling His followers where all the bad stuff comes from. He explicitly says that the thief does it, not Him.

> "The thief does not come except to steal, and to kill, and to destroy. I have come that they may have life, and that they may have it more abundantly." John 10:10 (NKJV)

However, Jesus does tell us to seek the Kingdom of God ***FIRST*** and all the things of life will take care of themselves. He has been talking about what to eat, drink, and the clothing that we wear. The basic necessities of life.

> "Seek first the kingdom of God and His righteousness, and all these things shall be added to you." Matthew 6:33 (NKJV)

But Jesus doesn't say don't take care of your financial and physical needs. He tells us to seek the kingdom of God first and foremost, then work on the other things. He does not say to neglect them. He tells us not to worry about them.

> "Then He said to His disciples, 'Therefore I say to you, do not worry about your life, what you will eat; nor about the body, what you will put on. Life is more than food, and the body is more than clothing. Consider the ravens, for they neither sow nor reap, which have neither storehouse nor barn; and God feeds them. Of how much more value are you than the birds? And which of you by worrying can add one cubit to his stature? If you then are not able to do the least, why are you anxious for the rest? Consider the lilies, how they grow: they neither toil nor spin; and yet I say to you, even Solomon in all his glory was not arrayed like one of these. If then God so clothes the grass, which today is in the field and tomorrow is thrown into the oven, how much more will He clothe you, O you of little faith? And do not seek what you should eat or what you should drink, nor have an anxious mind. For all these things the nations of the world seek after, and your Father knows that you need these things. But seek the kingdom of God, and all these things shall be added to you."
> Luke 12:22-29 (NKJV)

So if we look at all these scriptures as a whole, money is not a bad thing. It's actually a very good thing. Our view of money (or somebody else's view that has been taught to us) can be out of balance. Yes, the true riches in Jesus are spiritual, the fruit of the Spirit, the Kingdom of God, but He doesn't deny our need for money. Goodness! He can put temple tax money in a fishes' mouth!

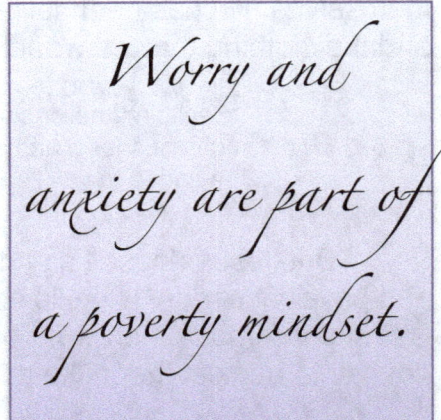

Worry and anxiety are part of a poverty mindset.

He can and will provide for us, but we must rid ourselves of all the negative ideologies we've been taught about money. If we are strapped for cash and cannot pay our bills, then worry sets in and all our focus is on how we can cover our bills this month. That is NOT seeking the Kingdom first and I don't believe God wants any of His children living this way. This is a poverty mindset—not enough, always looking at the lack—and this is NOT the mindset of Jesus!

Joy and peace are part of an abundance mindset.

I would love for the idea of the abundance of God to be ingrained in you! If one can't pay their bills or they have just enough to cover their bills (which is better than not being able to pay their bills!), they don't have anything left to help others. They may have a good eye and want to be generous, but are unable to do so because of their financial means. Time and things, yes. Money, no.

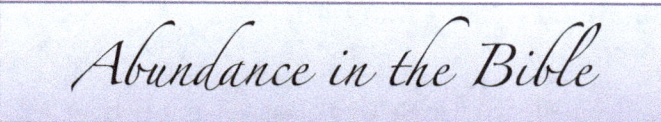

We've already looked at John 10:10 where Jesus said that He came that we might have an abundant life. The Psalmist talks about the abundance of the path of God, His table spread before us, and yes, even prosperity!

> "You crown the year with Your goodness,
> and Your paths drip with abundance."
> Psalm 65:11 (NKJV)

> "You prepare a table before me in the
> presence of my enemies; You anoint
> my head with oil; my cup runs over."
> Psalm 23:5 (NKJV)

> "He shall be like a tree planted by the
> rivers of water, that brings forth its fruit
> in its season, whose leaf also shall not
> wither; and whatever he does shall
> prosper." Psalm 1:3 (NKJV)

> "They are abundantly satisfied with the
> fullness of Your house, and You give them
> drink from the river of Your pleasures."
> Psalm 36:8 (NKJV)

In the Old Testament, there is a blessing that comes with keeping the Law. In many cases, it was kind of like an if-then clause. If you do this, then God will do this. We see time and again where Israel stopped following the Law, then other countries would come and overcome them. Eventually, a good king would come to reign and Israel would get free from their enemies. A time of prosperity would come. Then the cycle would begin again. Israel would stop following the Law, and they would be beaten by another country. Let's look at a few of the blessings that God had in store for the Israelites *if* they walked with Him.

"And you shall remember the Lord your God, for it is He who gives you power to get wealth, that He may establish His covenant which He swore to your fathers as it is this day." Deut 8:18 (NKJV)

"Therefore keep the words of this covenant, and do them, that you may prosper in all that you do." Deut 29:9 (NKJV)

"The Lord your God will make you abound in all the work of your hand, in the fruit of your body, in the increase of your livestock, and in the produce of your land for good. For the Lord will again rejoice over you for good as He rejoiced over your fathers, if you obey the voice of the Lord your God, to keep His commandments and His statutes which are written in this Book of the Law, and if you turn to the Lord your God with all your heart and with all your soul." Deut 30: 9-10 (NKJV)

"This Book of the Law shall not depart from your mouth, but you shall meditate in it day and night, that you may observe to do according to all that is written in it. For then you will make your way prosperous, and then you will have good success." Joshua 1:8 (NKJV)

"And keep the charge of the Lord your God; to walk in His ways, to keep His statutes, His commandments, His judgments, and His testimonies, as it is written in the Law of Moses, that you may prosper in all that you do and wherever you turn;"   1Kings 2:3 (NKJV)
(King David to his son Solomon)

> "For I know the thoughts that I think toward
> you, says the Lord, thoughts of peace and
> not of evil, to give you a future and a hope."
> Jeremiah 29:11 (NKJV)

> "The blessing of the Lord makes one rich,
> and He adds no sorrow with it." Proverbs 10:22 (NKJV)

At the time of Jesus, a common thought was that wealthy people got that way because God had specifically blessed them because they were following His Law. It's fairly obvious in reading through the Gospels that many of the wealthy people that Jesus interacted with had hearts that were not following after God.

Let me remind you that because of Jesus' finished work on the cross and His resurrection, we are in a whole new ballgame! We are seated with Him in heavenly places. If that's not a place of abundance, well, I don't know what is! Here are some abundance Scriptures from our whole new ballgame testament!

> "Beloved, I pray that you may prosper in all
> things and be in health just as your soul
> prospers." 3 John 2 (NKJV)

> "Give and it will be given to you: good measure,
> pressed down, shaken together, and running
> over will be put into your bosom. For with the
> same measure that you use, it will be measured
> back to you." Luke 6: 38 (NKJV)

> "And my God shall supply all your need
> according to His riches in glory by Christ
> Jesus." Phil 4:19 (NKJV)

It's interesting to note that most of the abundance scriptures in the New Testament are on the true riches in Christ. If we follow Him with all our hearts, the things of this world will naturally follow. Because we're following Him with all our hearts, we really don't mind if they happen or not. We are satisfied in Him. We have a good eye. We are generous, loving people. But the Word is clear that the things of the world that we need will come.

Remember what Jesus said in John 10:10, that He came to give us an abundant life— spiritually and physically.

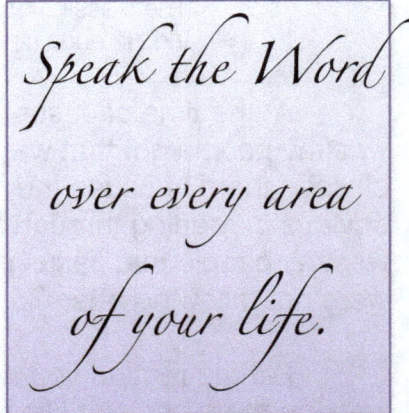

Speak the Word over every area of your life.

If, as you've read these scriptures, you've had any thoughts or feelings that you wish that these verses would happen to you, please keep a list of them with you and read them until they become a part of you. As you are able to change any lack, miserly, poverty thoughts you have held about money and replace them with the abundant life thoughts of Jesus, your life will change. Let's go back to our poverty mindset/abundant mindset scale and look at it only in terms of finances.

Poverty Mindset		Abundant Mindset
0	50	100

Where are you on this scale with the following thoughts?

1) Money is bad.
2) Money is a useful tool.

3) Money is an idol to be gotten rid of.
4) There is plenty of money to go around.
5) If I seek the Kingdom of God first, He will provide all my needs.
6) I give of my money and time freely because I want to.
7) I give of my money and time because I feel guilty.

Let's read again Jesus' words in Luke and keep in mind the good eye analogy.

> "Give, and it will be given to you: good
> measure, pressed down, shaken together,
> and running over will be put into your bosom.
> For with the same measure that you use, it
> will be measured back to you." Luke 6:38 (NJKV)

Are you seeing a pattern here? If you have found yourself on the poverty side of the scale, ask the Lord to help your unbelief. Ask Him to help you to believe that He wants you to have an abundant life in all areas. If, on the other hand, you've found yourself on the abundance side of the scale, ask Him where you could improve in this area. It could be working on more fruit of the Spirit in your life or more giving of time or money.

Practicing His Presence

1) Read the parable of the talents. Matthew 25: 14-30

2) Am I truly grateful for the things and people I have in my life right now? If my life were to remain exactly the same, would I still be grateful?

3) Where does a poverty mindset live in my life? Where do I complain? What can I do to change this area in my life?

4) Many of the scriptures caution us to be careful how we hear things. I believe it's talking about what we take in to ourselves. Think about news and social media. Negativity sells. What am I doing to either limit or counteract the negativity that I encounter throughout the day? GIGO— garbage in, garbage out

5) Pray for an abundant mindset. "Father God, I ask to be an abundant mindset person, just like You! You are an abundant God. I do truly believe this, in Jesus name, so be it!"

6) Do you have a good eye?

7) Pick you favorite verse from the Abundance in the Bible section and memorize it.

Notes

Chapter 9
Living in His Presence

As followers of Jesus, we need to have His perspective, not only on our lives, but on life in general. How do we, and can we, see life from God's perspective? In this chapter, we shall look at scriptures that speak about living in God's presence, some of which you've become well acquainted with by now. We shall discuss practical ways to implement these ideas into our lives. We will also continue looking at our position of being seated with Him in the Heavenly realm and what that means for us. We have God's perspective on our lives! We will delve into Jesus as our High Priest. We shall learn that Jesus made us kings and priests to the Most High God and what that means!

We can grow in our faith.

We can grow in our faith for answered prayer.

As we grow in our relationship with Jesus, our faith begins to grow. As we read His Word and get a greater understanding of God, our faith begins to grow. As we begin to know who we are in Christ, our faith begins to grow. As we see ourselves through God's eyes, our faith begins to grow. And grow. And GROW! Those little mustard seed sprouts become a forest and we start seeing our prayers get answered over and over and over. That forest of faith trees continues to reproduce seeds of faith so that our faith becomes endless. In our faith, we understand that God's abundance and abilities are infinite and it is His good pleasure to answer our prayers!

Life in Jesus

There is no joy nor satisfaction that can compare with our life journey with Jesus. The relationship time invested in learning to pray as Jesus taught is worth more than a million answered prayers. He invites us and, more importantly, He desires us to seek Him first in everything we do. As we journey with Him, we learn to live life with Him. The Word talks about an ancient path with Almighty God, a highway of holiness lighted by His Word. Walking on this path with Him is so amazing.

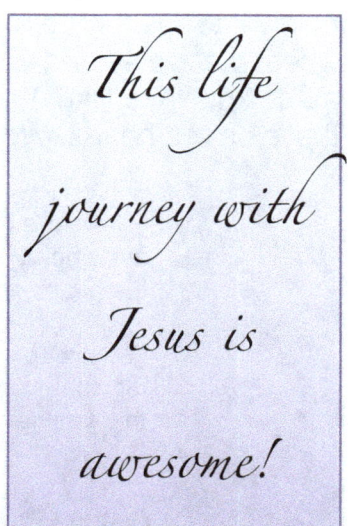

This life journey with Jesus is awesome!

"Stand in the crossroads and see, and ask for the ancient paths, where the good way is, and walk in it, then you will find rest for your souls." Jeremiah 6:16 (NKJV)

"A highway shall be there, and a road, and it shall be called the Highway of Holiness. The unclean shall not pass over it, but it shall be for others. Whoever walks the

road, although a fool, shall not go astray."
Isaiah 35:8 (NKJV)

"Your Word is a lamp to my feet and a light
to my path." Psalm 119:105 (NKJV)

So as we have learned, God, in His infinite wisdom and love, wanted family so much that He created the heavens and the earth. Then He created humans in His image to live with Him forever. Through the death and resurrection of Jesus, we now live in the kingdom of God. This is the same kingdom that Jesus preached about in His earthly ministry. We can live in our slice of life on earth as it is in heaven. He has raised us up and seated us with Him in the heavenly realm. We see ourselves as God sees us, blessed, redeemed, and utterly loved by Him! We come boldly into His throne room of grace—think about it! That's where we are seated with Him!—and we let our requests be made known to Him. We talk with Him about everything that's on our hearts. We couch our requests as Jesus taught.

"Therefore I say to you, whatever things you
ask when you pray, believe that you receive
them, and you will have them." Mark 11:24 (NKJV)

"This is the reason I urge you to boldly believe
for whatever you ask for in prayer—be convinced
that you have received it and it will be yours."
Mark 11:24 (TPT)

"For this reason I am telling you, whatever
things you ask for in prayer [in accordance
with God's will], believe [with confident trust]
that you have received them, and they will
be given to you." Mark 11:24 (AMP)

So we take the things we are praying about and we sit with them honestly before ourselves and the Lord. Do we really believe they will happen? If not, be totally honest with yourself, scale it back to the place where your insides cry out, "Yes! I do believe that!", and that's what you ask for. As that part of the prayer gets answered, then you add to it to the degree that you really believe it to be so. Ultimately, you'll get closer to the full answer that you desire.

A Child of the Most High God

As your forest of faith grows, as more of your prayers are answered, an amazing thing happens in your life. As you begin to understand and see more of the desires of your heart come to fruition, you become more confident of who you are in Jesus. You become more willing to enter boldly into the throne room of grace that was so eloquently written about. We enter boldly because through this journey of faith for answered prayer, we've come to know our Lord and Savior on a deeper level. There is no way not to grow in our relationship with Him as we learn to pray and receive answers to our prayers.

> "Seeing then that we have a great High Priest who has passed through the heavens, Jesus the Son of God, let us hold fast our confession. For we do not have a High Priest who cannot sympathize with our weaknesses, but was in all points tempted as we are, yet without sin. Let us therefore come boldly to the throne of grace, that we may obtain mercy and find grace to help in time need."
> Hebrews 4:14-16 (NKJV)

Learn to live in this space, seated with Him in the heavenly places. We've discussed this at length. Live your life with His perspective from this vantage point. This is where we live on earth as it is in heaven, whether we are sitting on our couches, cooking dinner, driving in our cars, whatever we may be doing, we are the connection between heaven and earth.

Our faith is all about Jesus. He is the Creator. He is the Redeemer. He died and rose again so that His life could dwell in us. We are His kids. Created in His image. The ones He saw worthy enough to create and to die for. He wants us to partner with Him in our journey of life. He wants us to grow in our faith. Part of this wonderful journey is to have faith in our faith in Him. We are children of the Most High God.

His Image Bearers

As we come to know Him more, our faith and trust in Him grows. As we come to know who we are in Him, the awesomeness of the finished work of the cross and His resurrection begins to dawn on us. At creation, God gave men and women authority over His creation.

> "Then God blessed them, and God said to them, 'Be fruitful and multiply; fill the earth and subdue it; have dominion over the fish of the sea, over the birds of the air, and over every living thing that moves on the earth.'"
> Genesis 1: 2 (NKJV)

Two short chapters later, we see that the woman was deceived about eating the forbidden fruit of the Tree of the Knowledge of Good and Evil. Her husband did not stop her. As far as we know from this story, he did not even try to stop her. When he saw that she didn't die, he ate the fruit also. By going against what God had told them specifically not to do, they gave their God-given dominion of the earth over to the serpent who had tempted Eve.

> "Then to Adam He said 'Because you
> have heeded the voice of your wife, and
> have eaten from the tree of which I
> commanded you, saying, 'You shall not
> eat of it': Cursed is the ground for your sake; in
> toil you shall eat of it all the days of your
> life. Both thorns and thistles it shall bring
> forth for you, and you shall eat the herb
> of the field. In the sweat of your face you
> shall eat bread till you return to the ground,
> for out of it you were taken; for dust you
> are and to dust you shall return.'"
>
> Genesis 3: 17-19 (NKJV)

The curse came upon creation, and we know that death began in their bodies. The Roman soldiers fashioned a cross of thorns and placed it upon Jesus' head. Thorns were the first sign of the curse that is mentioned. The crown of thorns was both a literal and a symbolic sign of the curse being placed on Jesus. His death and resurrection redeemed humans from the curse. After His resurrection and before His ascension Jesus gave the great commission to His Image Bearers.

> "And Jesus came and spoke to them,
> saying, "All authority has been given to
> Me in heaven and on earth. Therefore go
> and make disciples of all nations, baptizing
> them in the name of the Father and of the

Son and of the Holy Spirit and teaching them to obey everything I have commanded you. And surely I am with you always, to the very end of the age.'"
Matthew 28: 18-20 (NKJV)

Jesus was and is and always shall be the victor! He took back the authority of all of heaven and of all of earth. The Passion Translation says, "All authority of the universe has been given to me." Of course it has! He created the universe and He redeemed the universe. And we, as His image bearers, carry His authority in us. Through His presence dwelling in us we are victorious, too!

Jesus became a curse for us so that we might become the righteousness of God in Him.

The glory of Almighty God is inside of us!

As His image bearers, we notably carry His authority, but we also carry His glory. Remember in His High Priestly Prayer in John 17, Jesus said, "The glory which I had with You before the world was I have given them." Think about that. The very glory of Almighty God dwells inside of us!

154

Kings and Priests

In the Old Testament, there was a very distinct line between the priests who made the sacrifices and the kings who ruled over Israel. God did not want the governmental authority to also have the priestly authority over His people. They were very separate entities and the king had to come to the priest to offer his sacrifices.

The very first king, King Saul, very early in his reign blurred these lines and God took the kingdom out of Saul's hand. The lineage of the kings of Israel would have come from King Saul if he had not offered sacrifices as a priest. Kings were not to be priests and the High Priest was not to be king.

> "'then I said, 'The Philistines will now come down on me at Gilgal, and I have not made supplication to the Lord.' Therefore I felt compelled, and offered a burnt offering.' And Samuel said to Saul, 'You have done foolishly. You have not kept the commandment of the Lord your God which He commanded you. For now the Lord would have established your kingdom over Israel forever. But now your kingdom shall not continue. The Lord has sought for Himself a man after His own heart, and the Lord has commanded him to be commander over His people, because you have not kept what the Lord commanded you.'"
>
> 1 Samuel 13: 12-14 (NKJV)

There was something about the shepherd boy, David, that tugged at the heart of God. Samuel anointed David king over Israel, but it took David a very long time to ascend the throne. We all know that David had his own issues, but somehow in the midst of all of that, David continued to be a man after God's own heart.

I want you to remember that we are in a whole new ballgame, okay? David prophesied about the coming Messiah in his songs. We have that Messiah living inside of us! There is a marvelous verse in one of Peter's letters that calls us a royal priesthood. The Passion Translation calls us priests who are kings! John, in his revelation, also calls us kings and priests. Now, think about it, kings of Israel were forbidden to be priests, but we are called kings and priests! All because of Jesus, the Messiah!

> "But you are a chosen generation, a royal priesthood, a holy nation, His own special people, that you may proclaim the praises of Him who called you out of darkness into His marvelous light;" 1 Peter 2:9 (NKJV)

> "But you are God's chosen treasure—priests who are kings, a spiritual "nation" set apart as God's devoted ones. He called you out of darkness to experience his marvelous light, and now he claims you as his very own. He did this so that you would broadcast his glorious wonders throughout the world." 1 Peter 2:9 (TPT)

> "and has made us kings and priests to His God and Father, to Him be glory and dominion forever and ever. Amen" Rev 1:6 (NKJV)

> "You have chosen us to serve our God and formed us into a kingdom of priests who reign on the earth." Rev 5: 10 (TPT)

As kings of the Most High God, Jesus has given us the right to use His authority in His name. What's His authority? In our Matthew Scripture, Jesus told His disciples, "All authority has been given to Me in heaven and on earth." All authority. Jesus is the King of kings. We are the kings that

He is King over! Isn't that magnificent? As a king of the Most High God, we have the right to use the authority of our King Jesus!

In the Old Testament, only the High Priest could go into the Holy of Holies and that only once a year. He had bells on the bottom of his robe and a rope tied around his ankle. If he went in and the proper sacrifice had not been made, the High Priest would have died. The bells would have ceased to ring. The other priests would have used the rope to pull him out from behind the veil.

As priests of the Most High God, we can come boldly into the throne of grace. Because Jesus was the perfect sacrificial lamb, all our sin is gone as though it never happened! Because of Jesus, we stand before God sinless. Because of Jesus, the One Who used to dwell in the Holy of Holies now lives inside of our mortal bodies. He is a treasure in our earthen vessels! Because of Jesus, we are kings and priests to the Most High God! We are His image bearers!

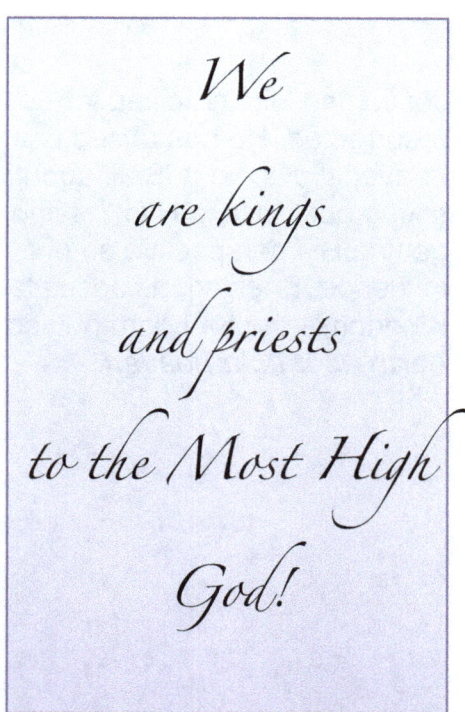

We are kings and priests to the Most High God!

This statement is both exhilarating and strikes fear at the core of our being! We carry His authority in us. As we understand His authority in us, then our faith in what He's done for us and what He wants to do through us grows. And finally, as we walk on this ancient pathway of faith, we begin

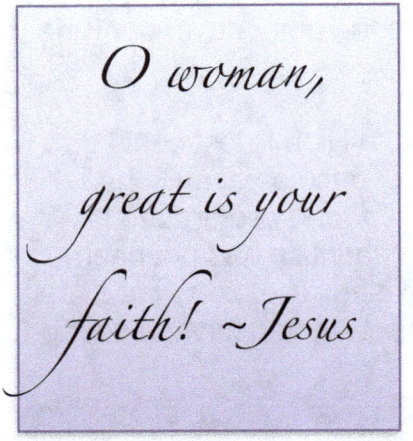

O woman, great is your faith! ~Jesus

to realize that our faith is growing. Then our belief in the faith within us grows. May Jesus marvel at your faith for answered prayer!

We've had a lot of practicing His presence ideas. I hope you've implemented some of them. Now it's time to bring everything into a cohesive whole. We have come full circle. It is all about Jesus and Him crucified for us. Not only crucified, but resurrected. He has raised us up and seated us with Him in heavenly places! It IS all about Jesus. For us, it is about us taking our place in Him, having the Mind of Christ, and getting His perspective on our lives and our spheres of influence. Seeking, as Jesus taught His disciples, His Kingdom—the Kingdom of God—to come in our lives **on earth as it is in heaven**.

Practicing His Presence

1) Take a look at the things you are praying for. Do you believe, really believe, that you have already received them?

2) Now see yourself sitting with Jesus in the heavenly places. Look at the things you are praying for. You are seated in heavenly places with Almighty God—the One Who spoke everything into existence! And you're there because He raised you up because He wanted you to sit with Him! Do those things delight your heart? If you delight yourself in God, He will give you the desires of your heart!

3) Think about the mustard seeds that you planted several chapters ago. Are you watering them with your faith? Have you seen any sprouts yet?

4) As you go about your day, start seeing your life with Jesus in the everyday happenings—a beautiful life!

5) Imagine yourself as both a royal king and a royal priest. You are the image bearer of the Most High God. If you could see yourself dressed in heaven's garments, the robes of kings and priests, what would you look like? Pretend that you have a crown in your hands. Now place it on your head.

Notes

Prayer List

Prayer List

"What honor you have given to men, created only a little lower than Elohim, crowned like kings and queens with glory and magnificence. You have relegated to them mastery over all You have made, making everything subservient to their authority, placing earth itself under the feet of Your Image-Bearers! All the created order and every living thing of the earth, sky, and sea —— the wildest beasts and all the sea creatures ——- everything is in submission to Adam's sons."

Psalm 8: 5-8 (TPT)

Bibliography

Chapman, Dr. Gary. *The 5 Love Languages: How to Express Heartfelt Commitment to Your Mate.* Manjul Publishing House, 2001.

Milne, A.A. *The House at Pooh Corner.* Dutton Books for Young Readers, 2018.

Smythe, Peter. "The Faith of God (God-kind of Faith)," The Mechanics of Faith. Hopefaithprayer.com

Webster, Noah. *Webster's New World Dictionary, Second College Edition.* Williams Collins Publishers, Inc. 1980.

Resources

Doug Addison   Inlight Connection DougAddison.com

Dr. Gary Chapman   5lovelanguages.com

Nancy Drew series by Carolyn Keen

Timothy Mackie and Jonathan Collins   bibleproject.com

Kristi McLelland   Jesus and Women - Bible Study
   lifeway.com

Regent University   regent.edu
1000 Regent University Drive
Virginia Beach, VA 23464

James Webb Space Telescope - NASA
webb.nasa.gov

Laura Taylor Cox was born in Nashville,TN and raised in Lewisburg. She earned her BS degree from Vanderbilt University and holds a Masters of Communications in Theater Arts from Regent University. While studying at Regent, she met her husband, Bill. They have been married over 40 years and have four children and 7 grandchildren.

Laura studied drama at the American Academy of Dramatic Arts in Los Angeles, then studied Shakespeare at the Royal Academy of Dramatic Art in London, England. She has had numerous roles in industrial films and videos. Laura has written, produced, directed and acted in many plays and sketches for her local churches over the years.

Laura has believed in Jesus since being a young child. When Laura was 17, she became an avid follower of Jesus and a student of the Bible. Her journey with Him over the last five decades had been an adventure of growing in the grace and knowledge of her Lord and Savior, Jesus, the Messiah.

www.thisdivinemystery.com
IG @laurataylorcox
FB - Laura Taylor Cox author
Laura@thisdivinemystery.com

www.ingramcontent.com/pod-product-compliance
Lightning Source LLC
Chambersburg PA
CBHW060526130626
46553CB00002B/663

* 9 7 9 8 9 8 8 9 2 8 9 2 8 *